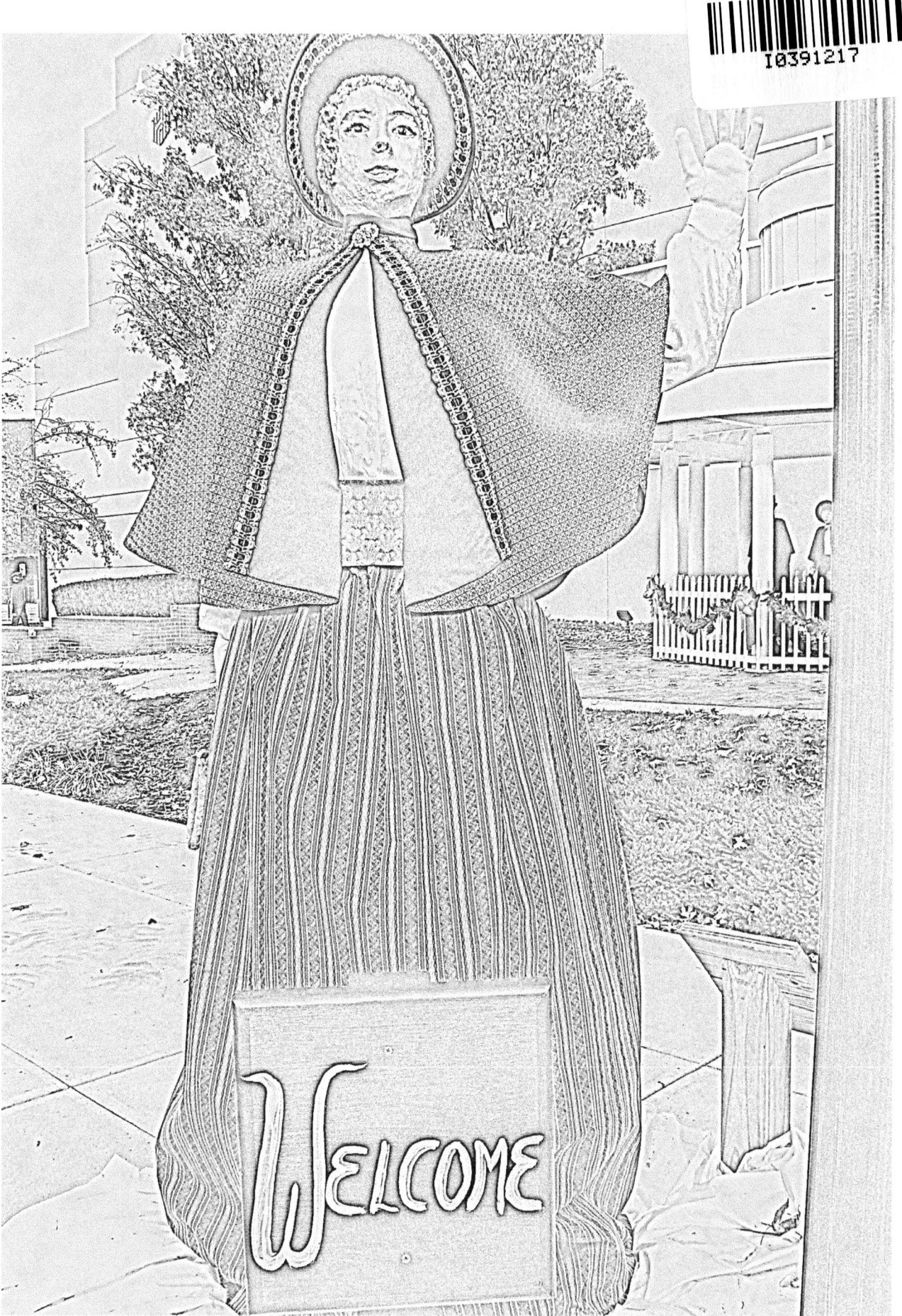

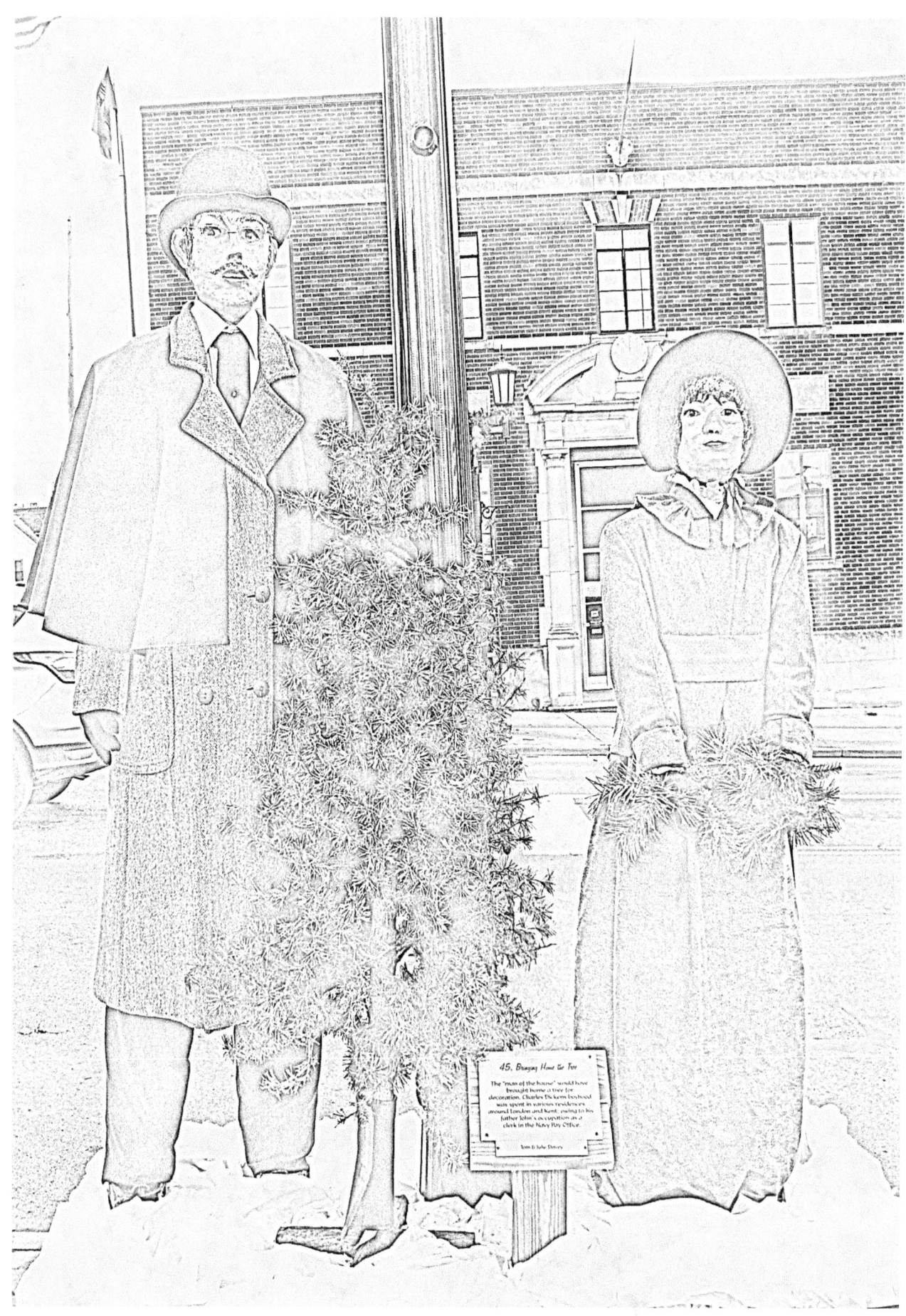

45, Bringing Home the Tree

The "man of the house" would have brought home a tree for decoration. Charles Dickens boyhood was spent in various residences around London and Kent, owing to his father John's occupation as a clerk in the Navy Pay Office.

Tom & Julie Denes

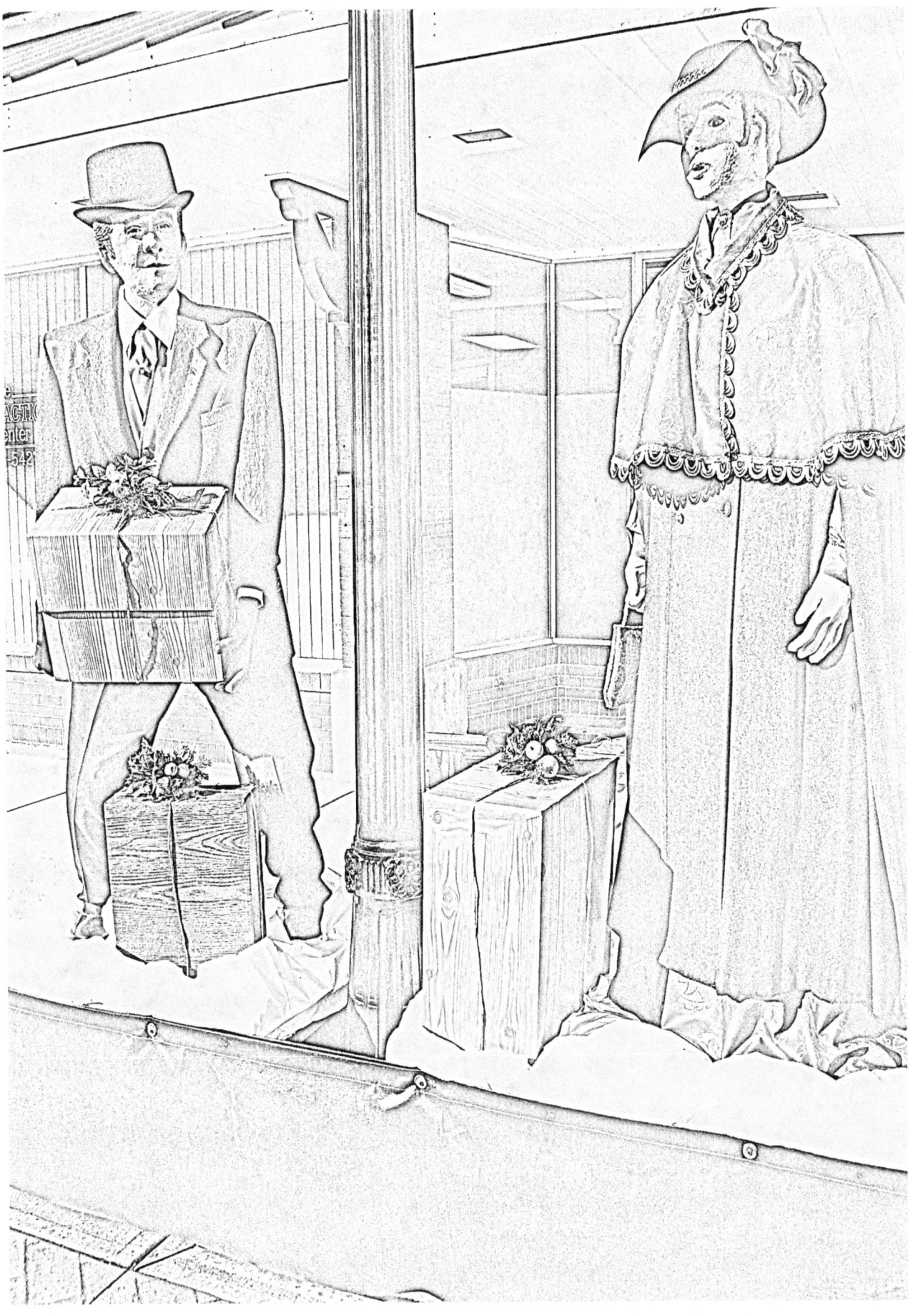

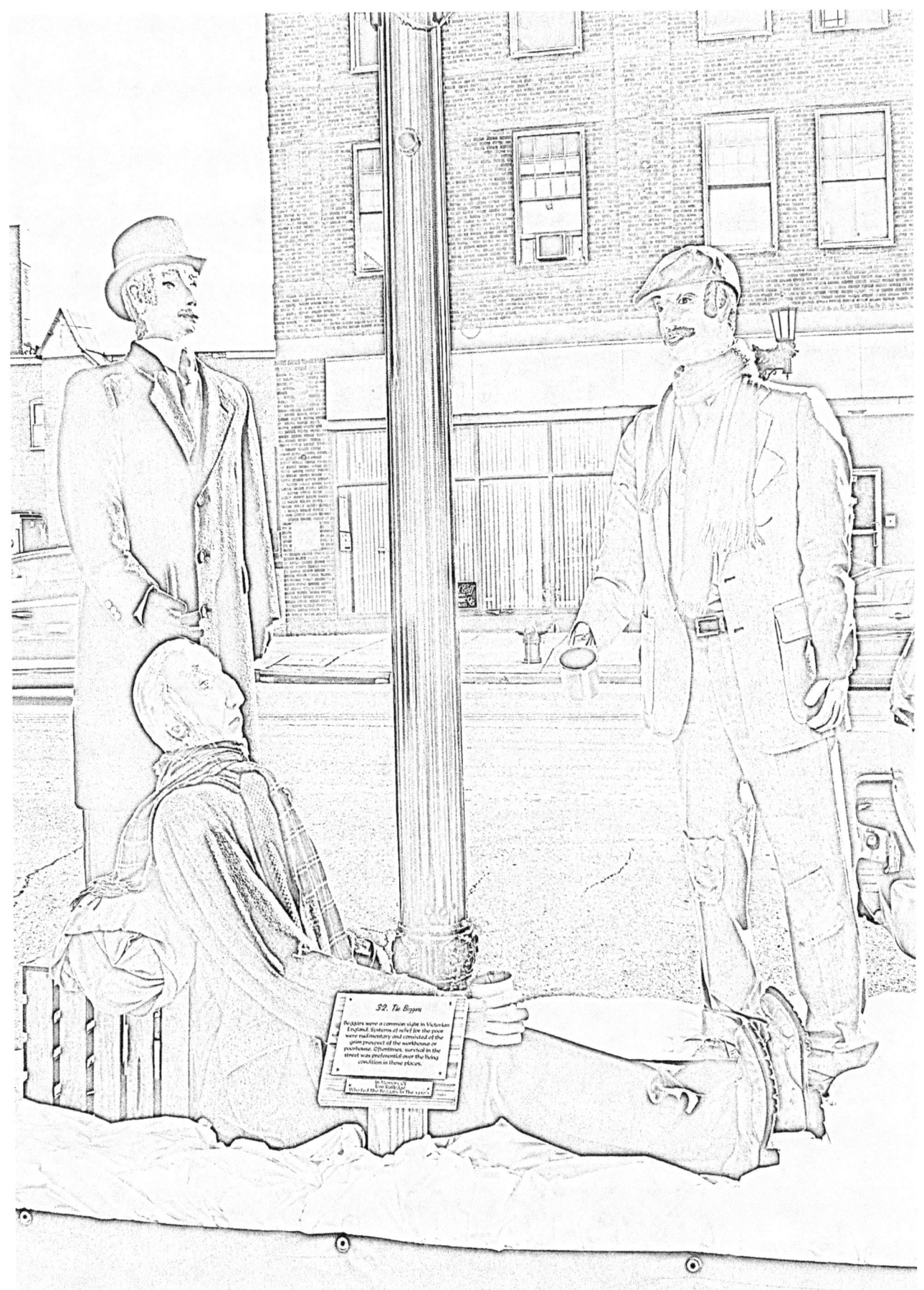

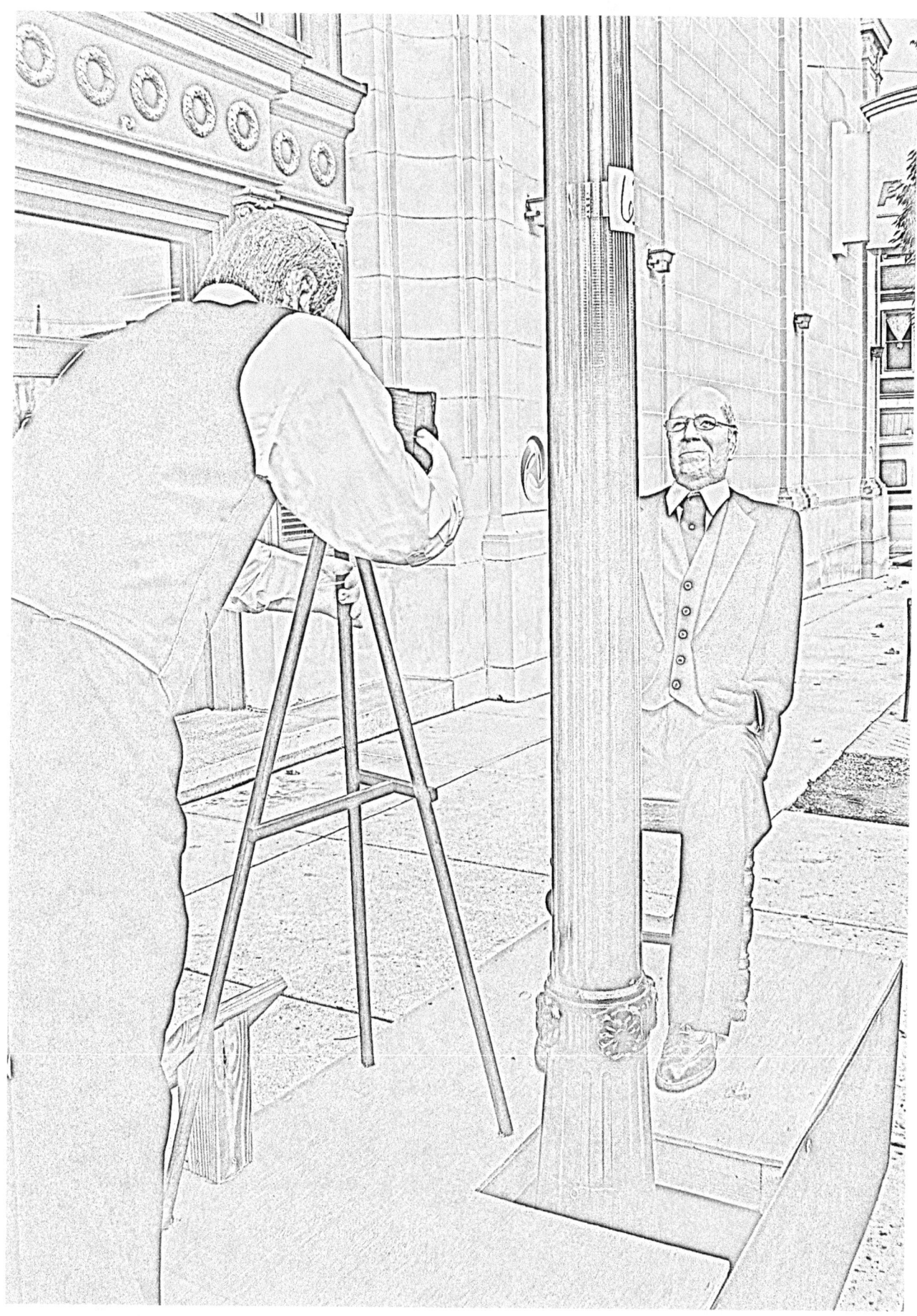

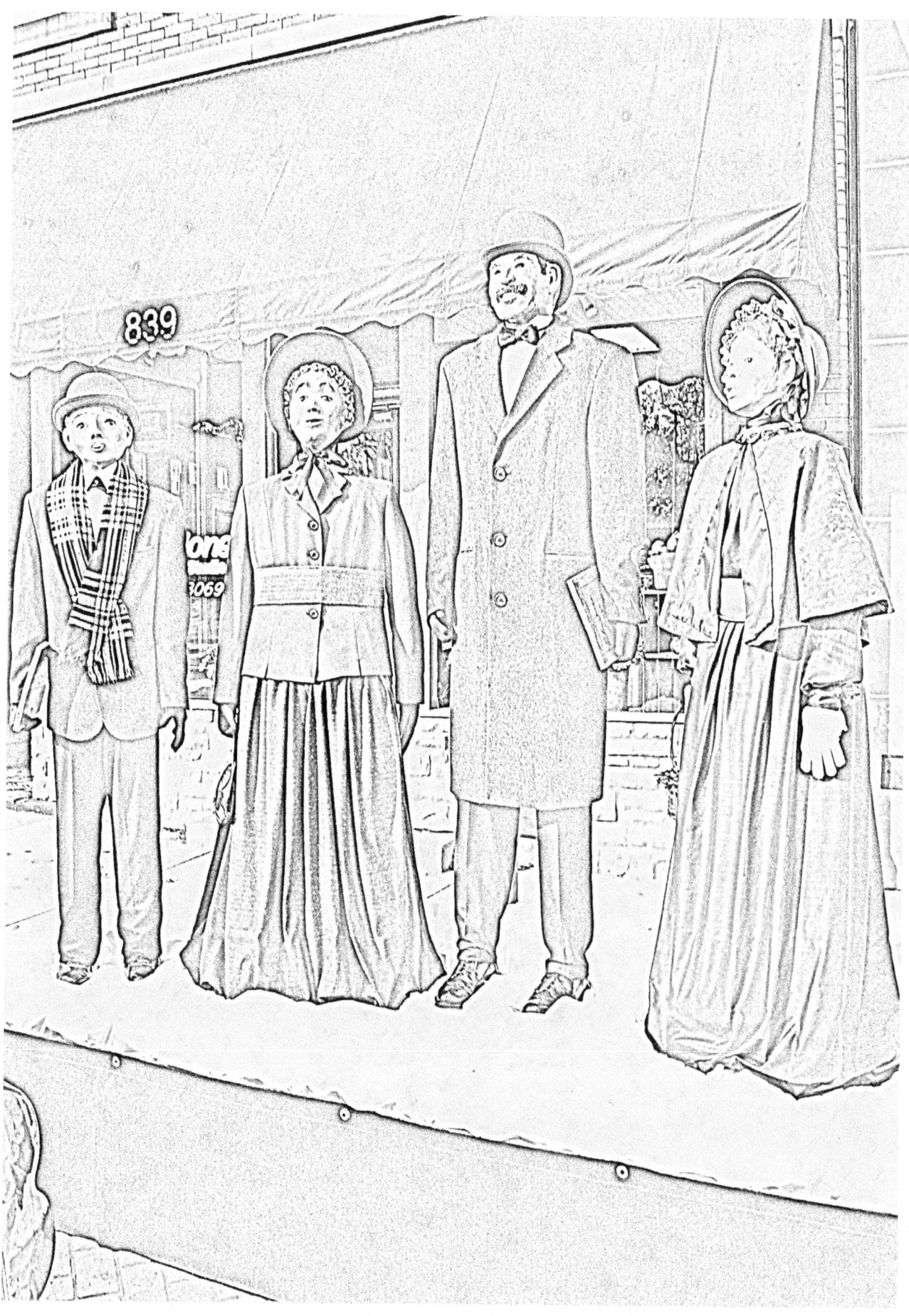

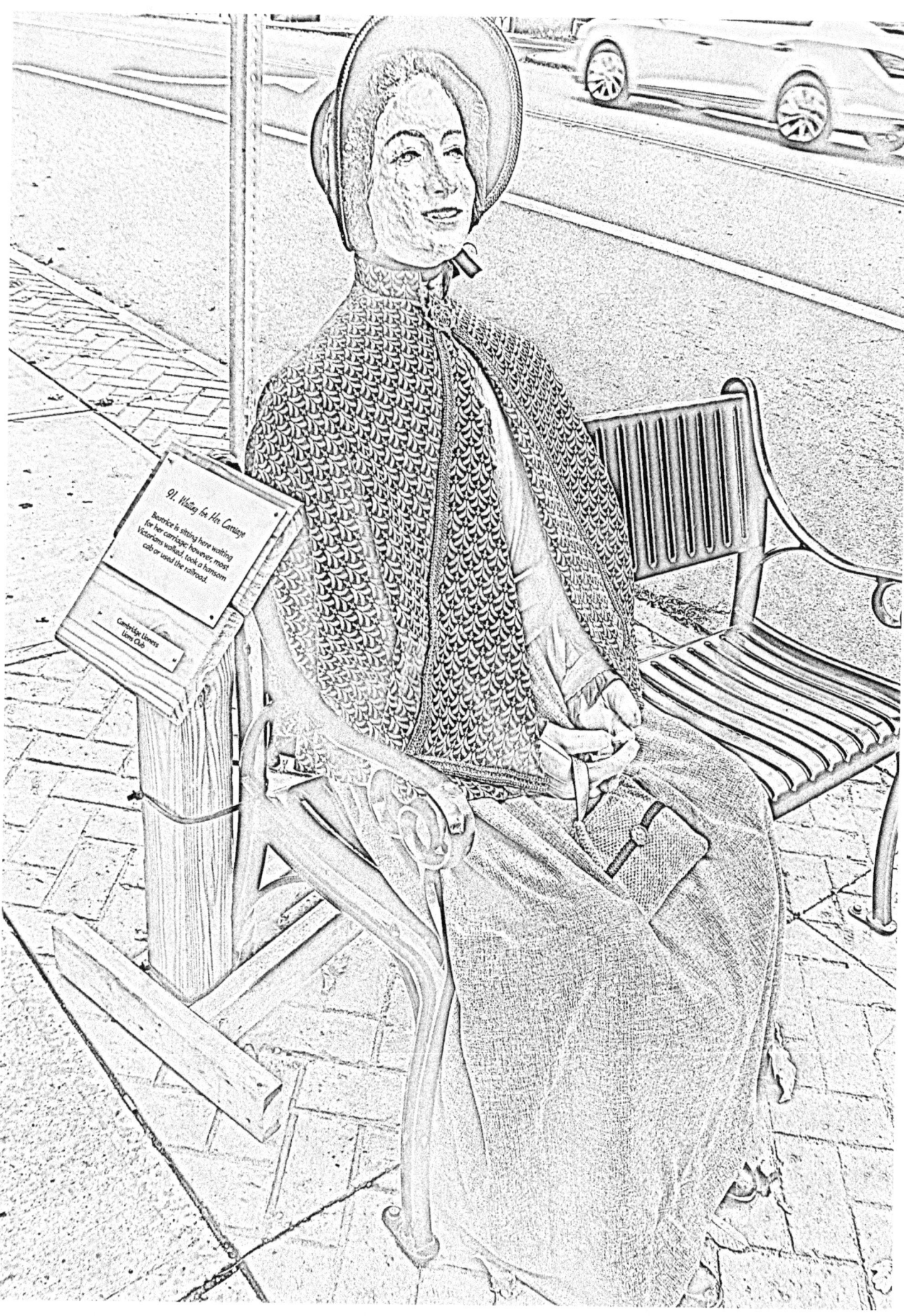

91. Waiting for Her Carriage

Beatrice is sitting here waiting
for her carriage; however, most
Victorians walked, took a hansom
cab or used the railroad.

Cambridge Lioness
Lions Club

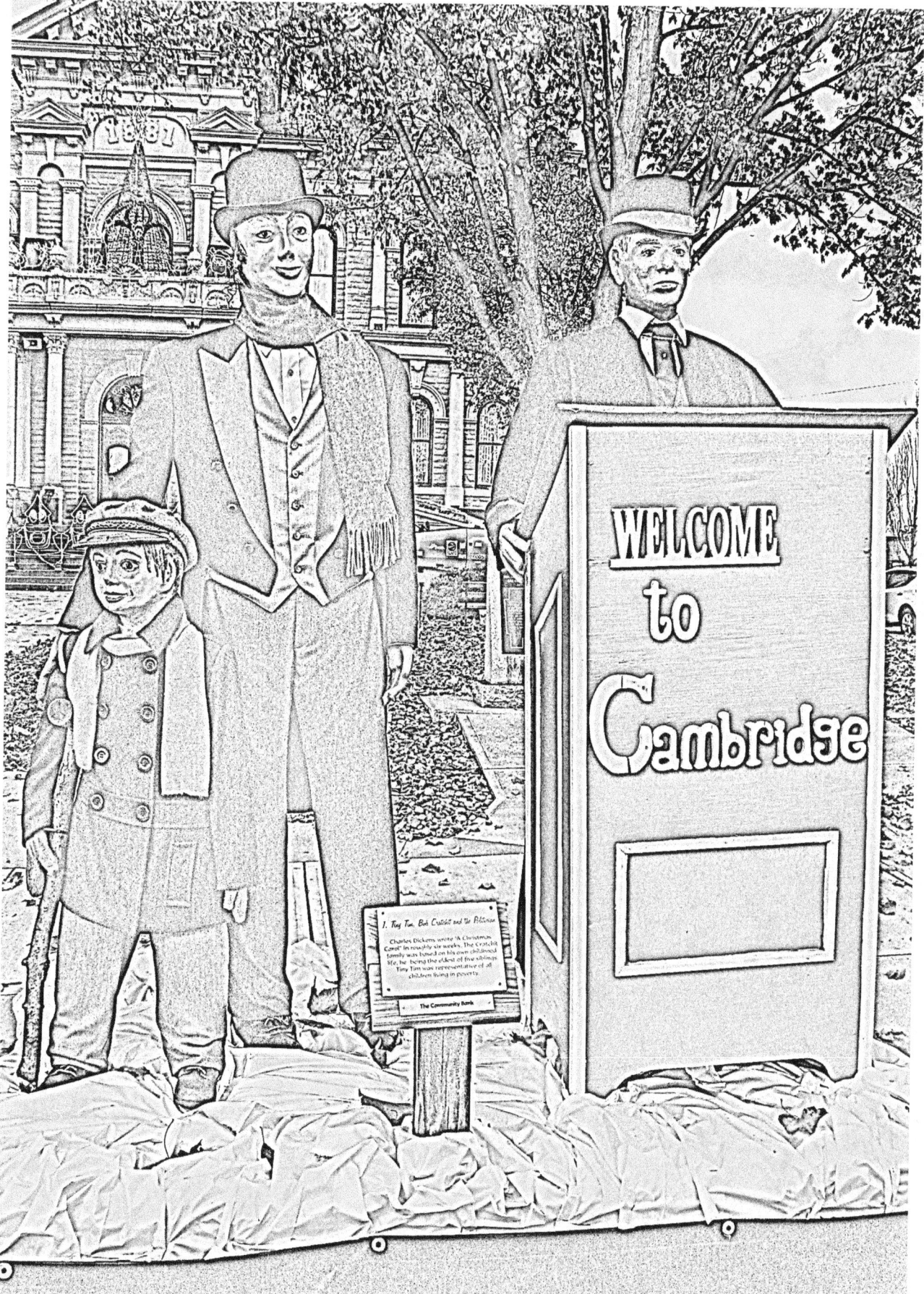

WELCOME
to
Cambridge

1. Tiny Tim, Bob Cratchit and the Petition

Charles Dickens wrote "A Christmas
Carol" in roughly six weeks. The Cratchit
family was based on his own childhood
life, he being the eldest of five siblings.
Tiny Tim was representative of all
children living in poverty.

The Community Bank

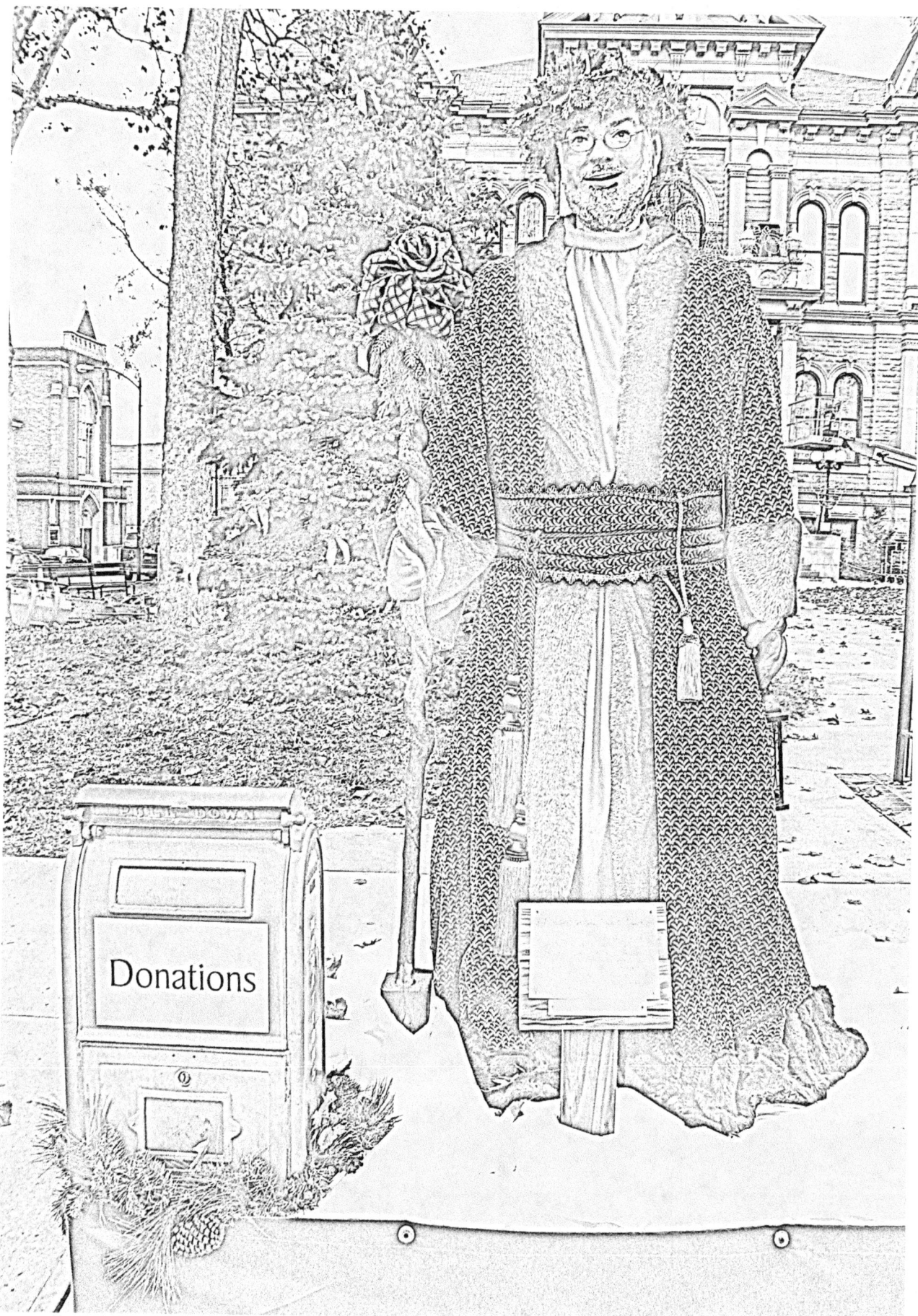

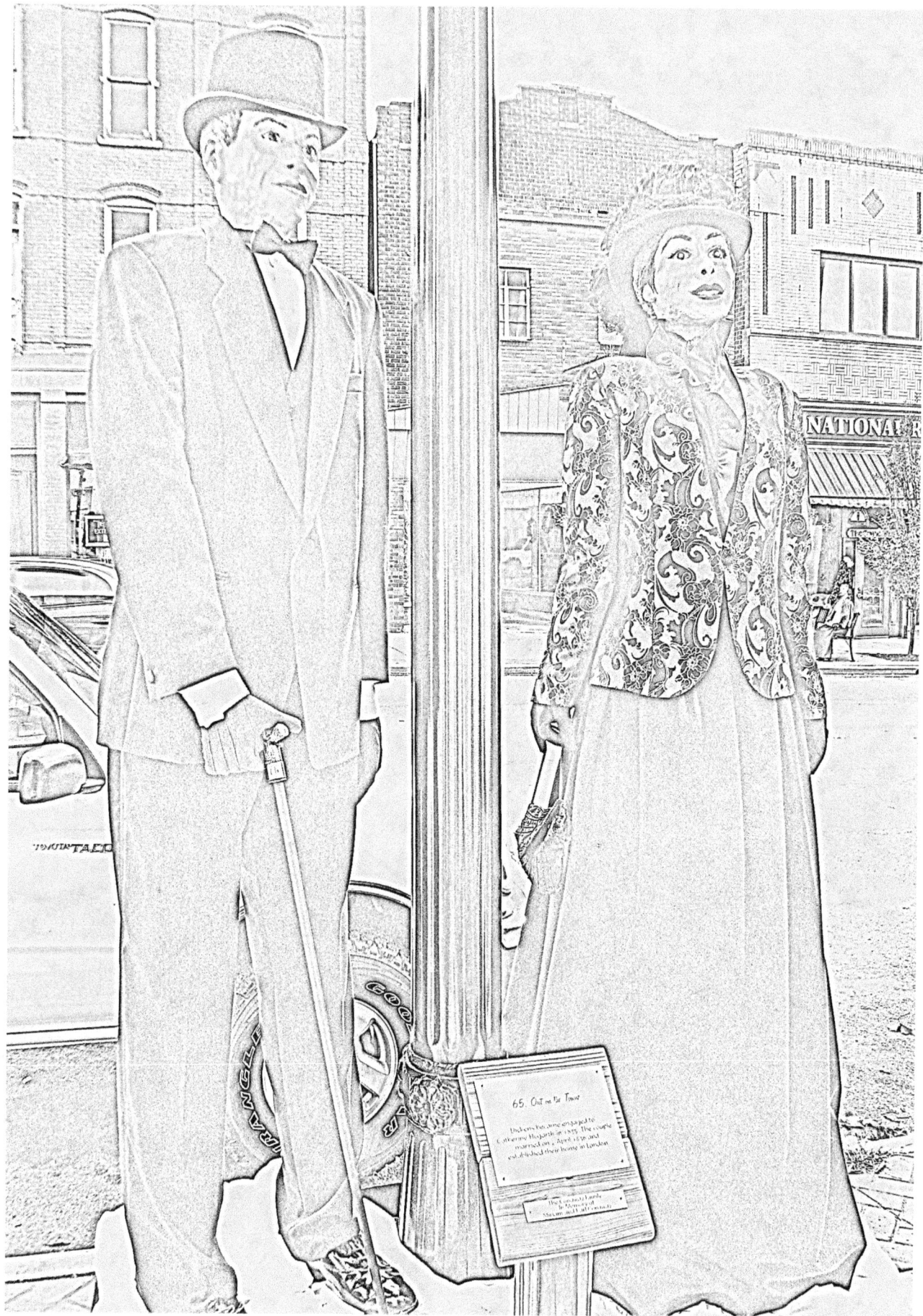

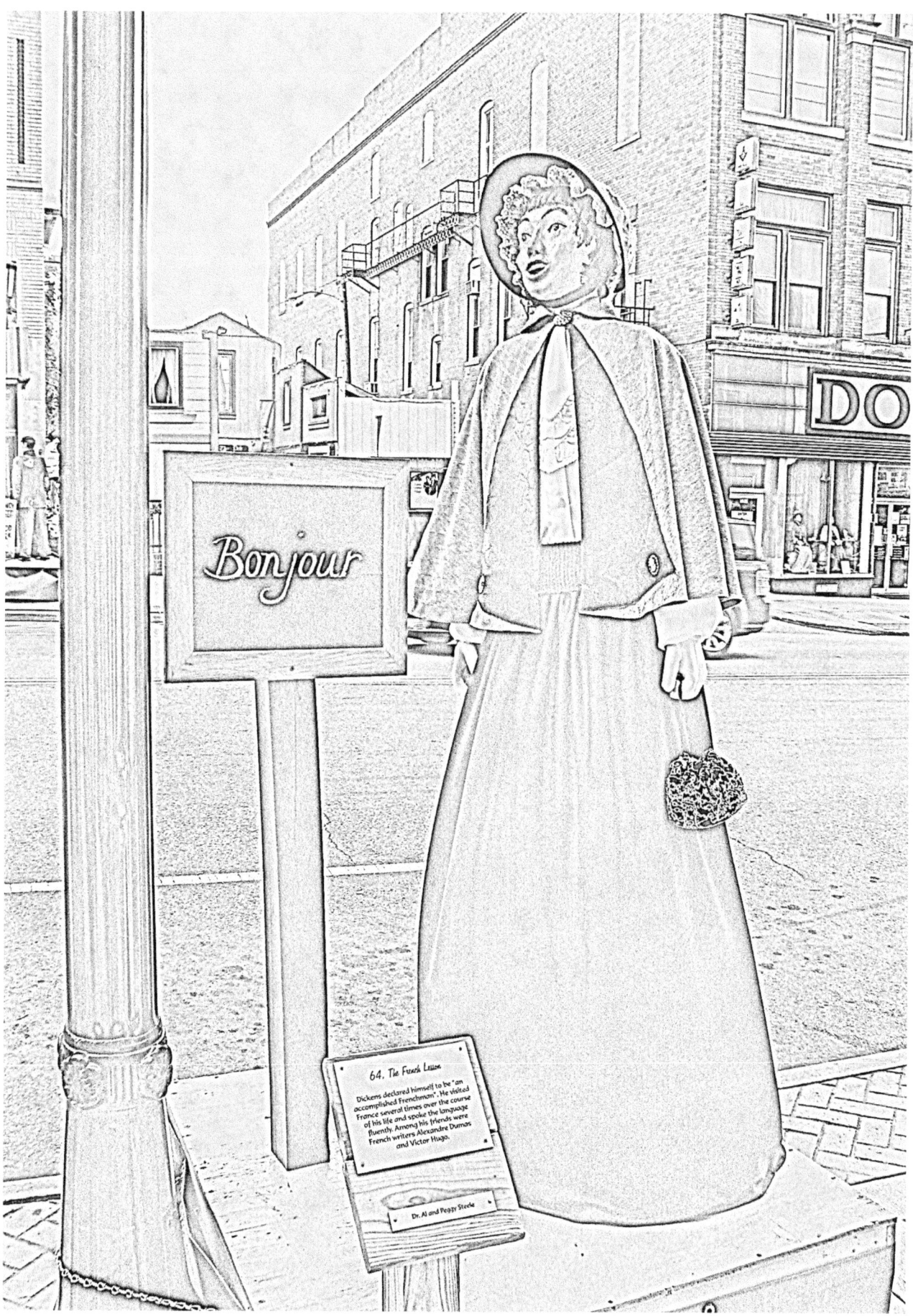

Bonjour

64. The French Lesson

Dickens declared himself to be "an accomplished Frenchman". He visited France several times over the course of his life and spoke the language fluently. Among his friends were French writers Alexandre Dumas and Victor Hugo.

Dr. Al and Peggy Steele

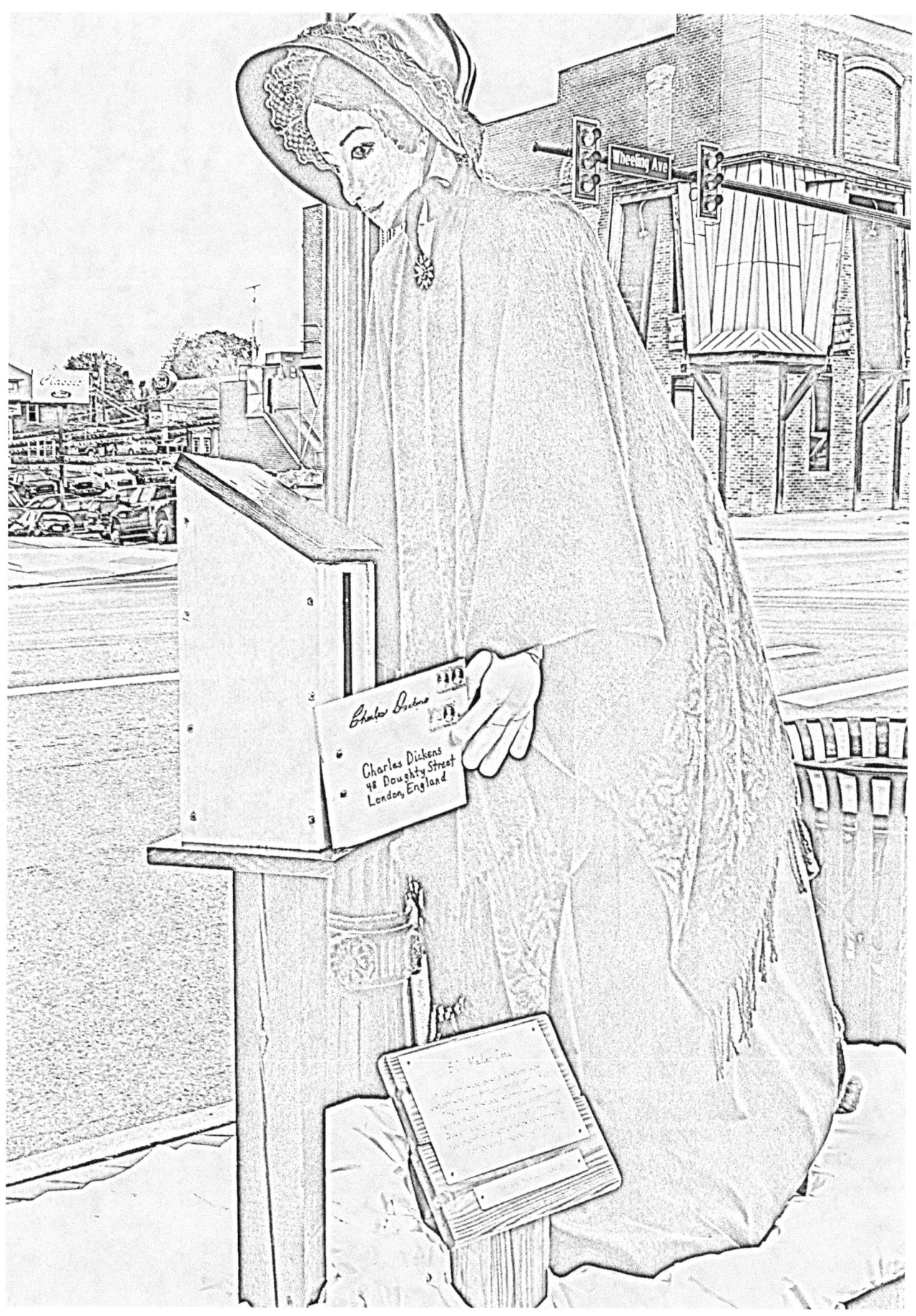

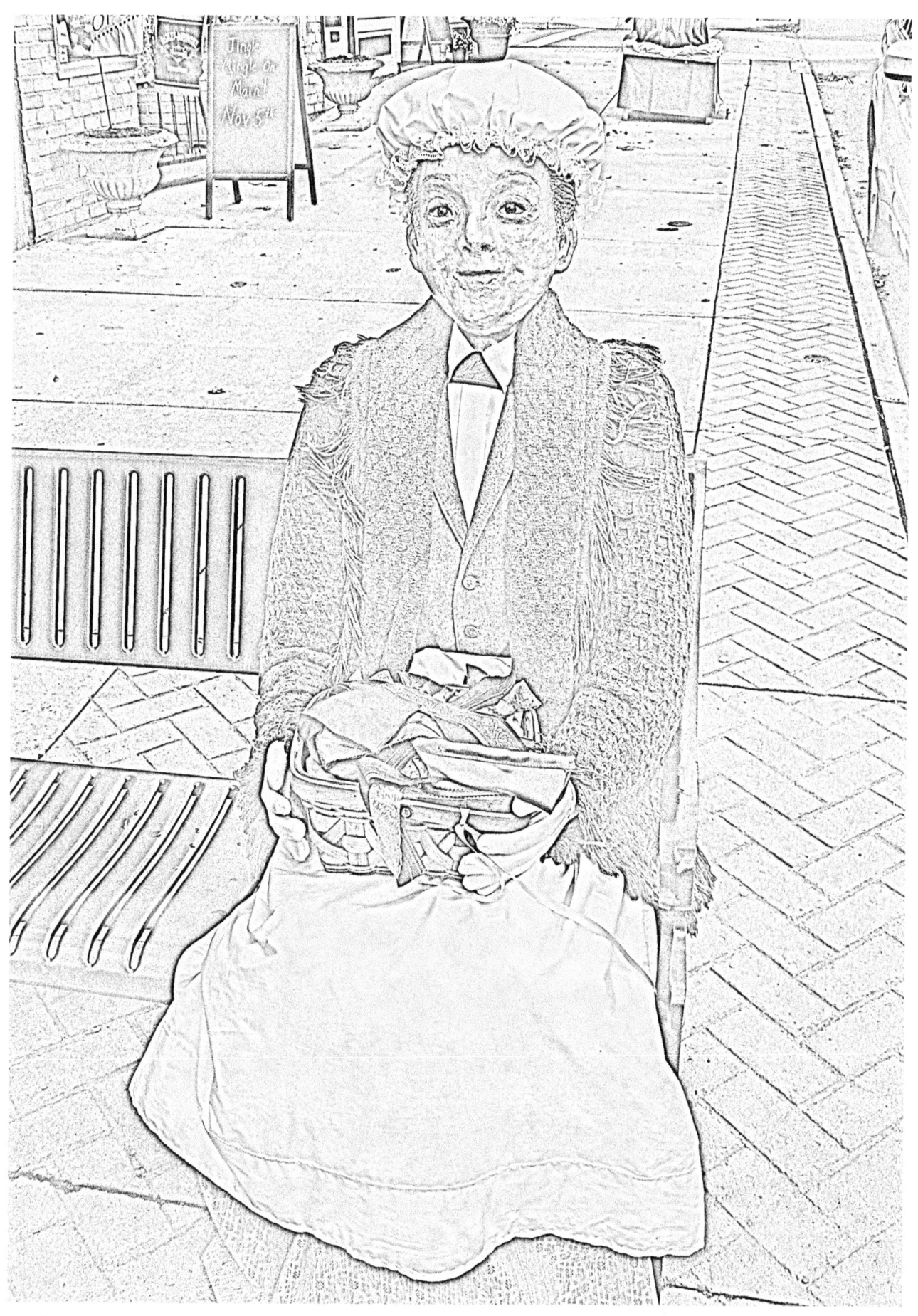

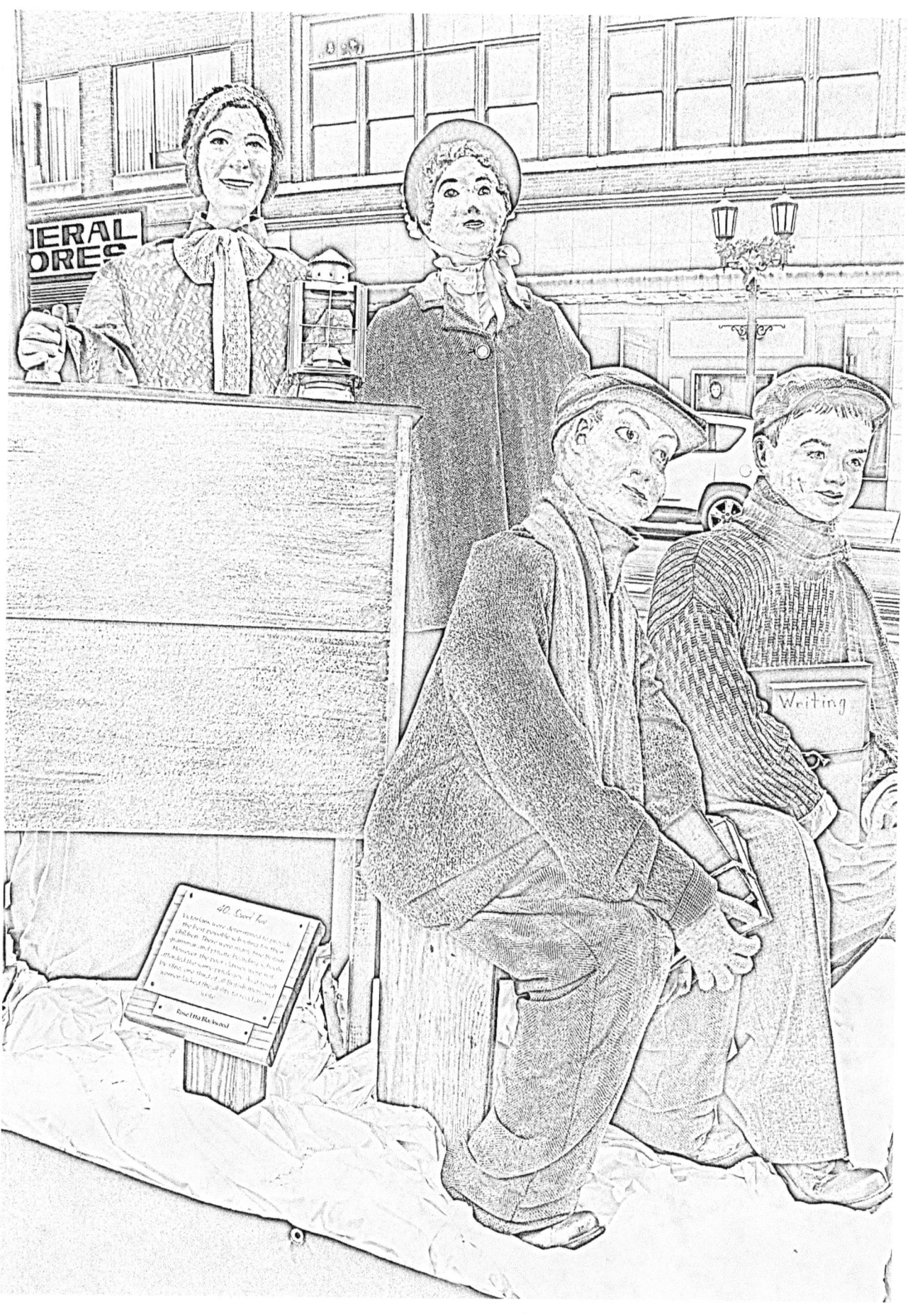

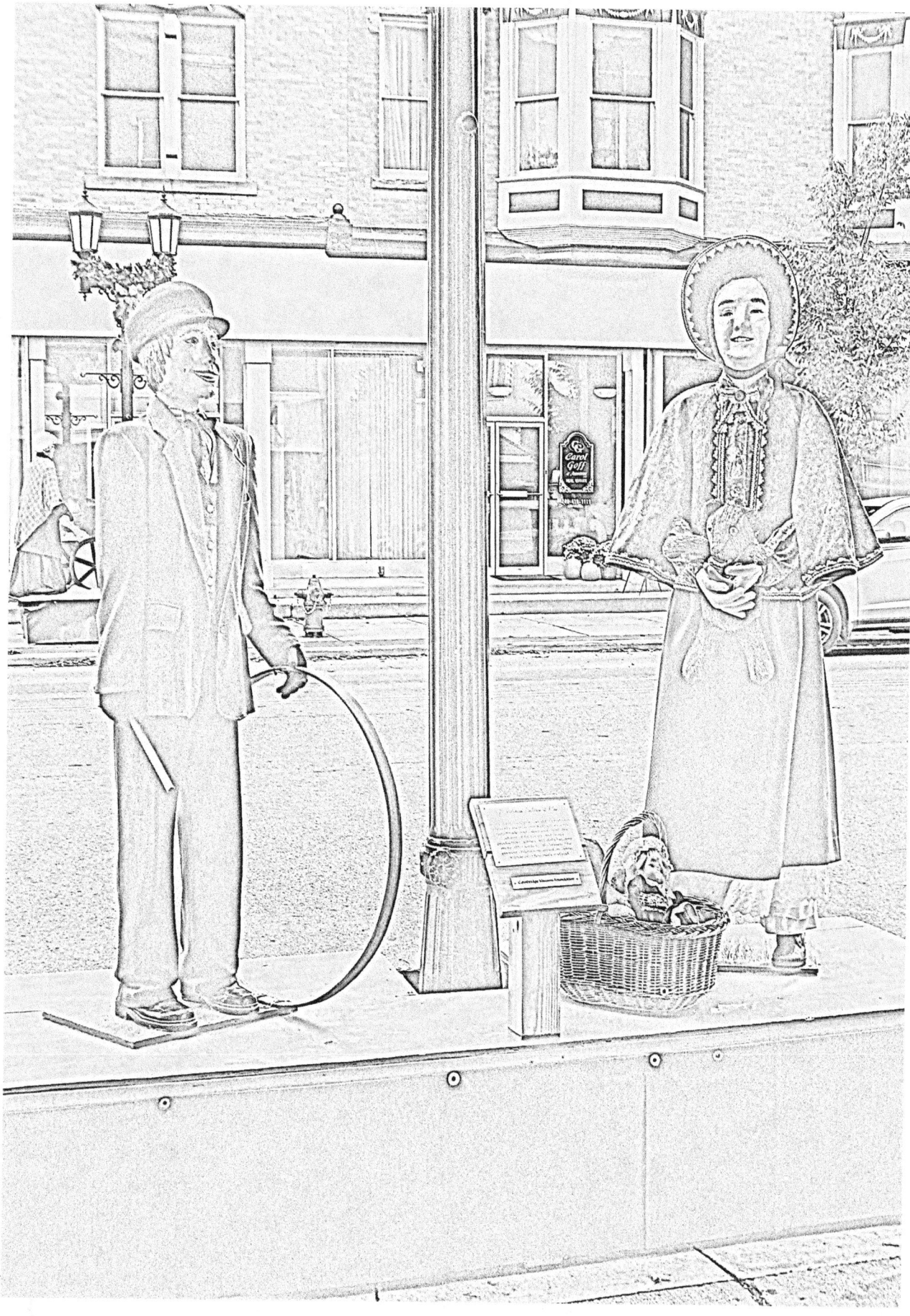

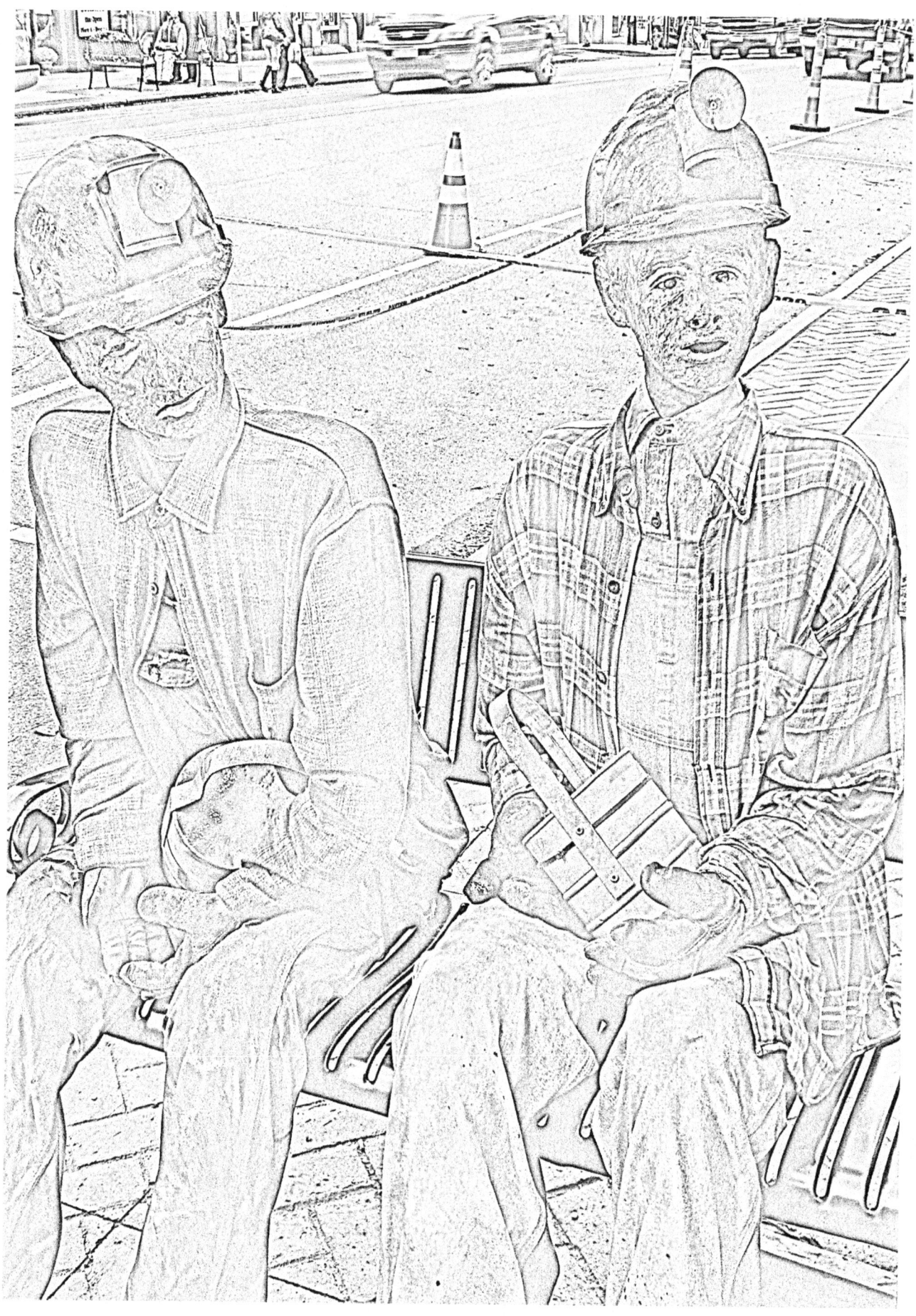

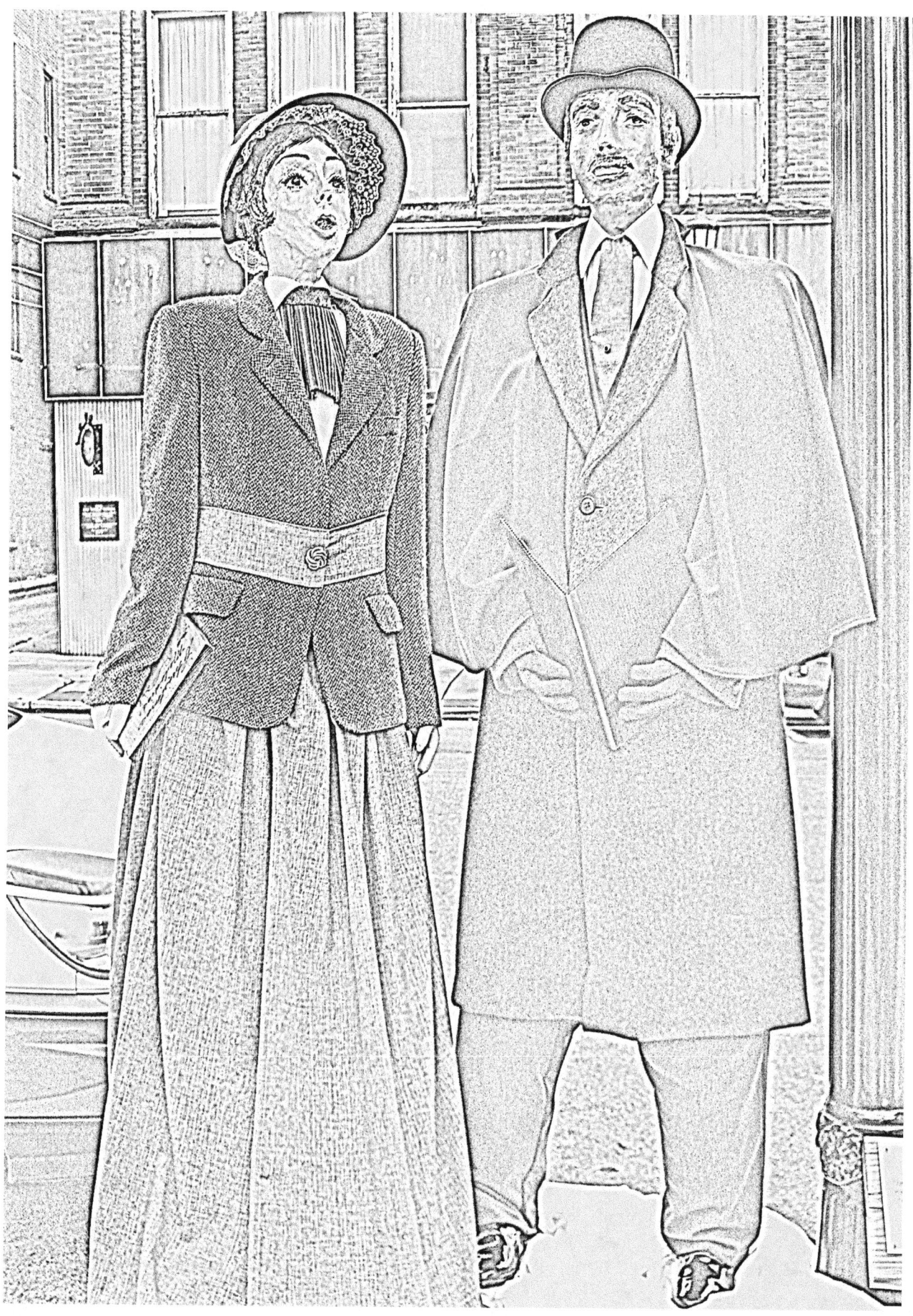

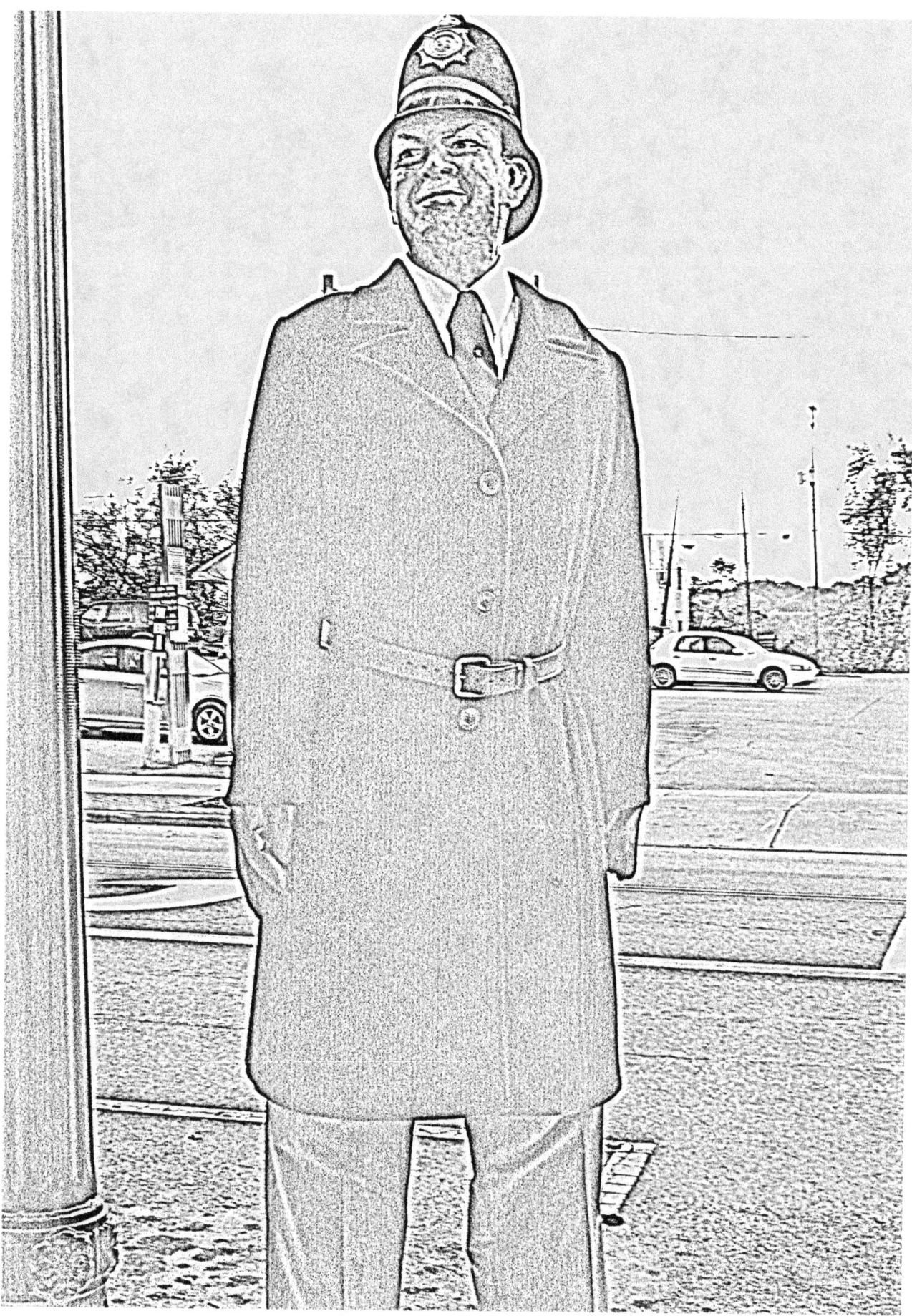

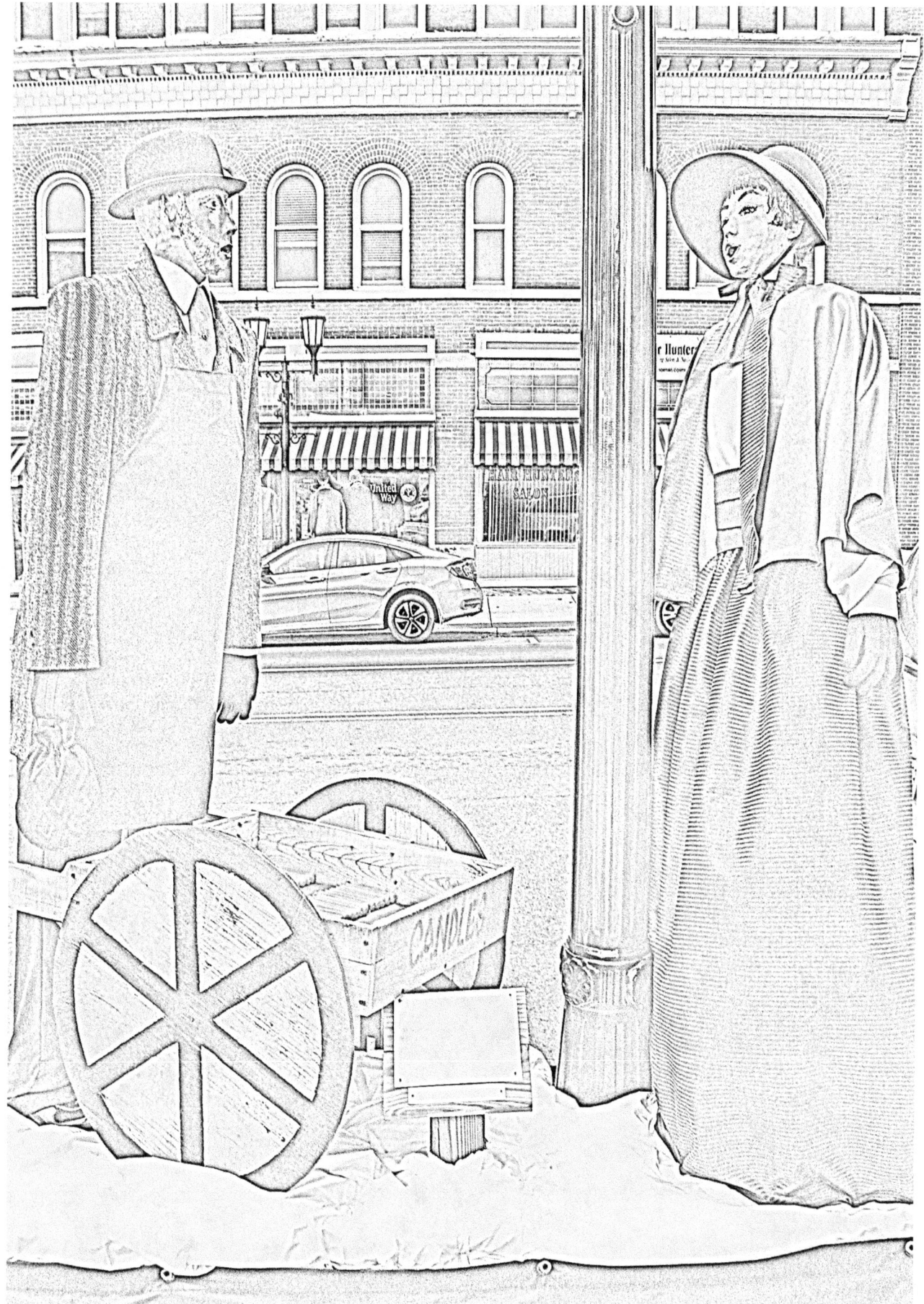

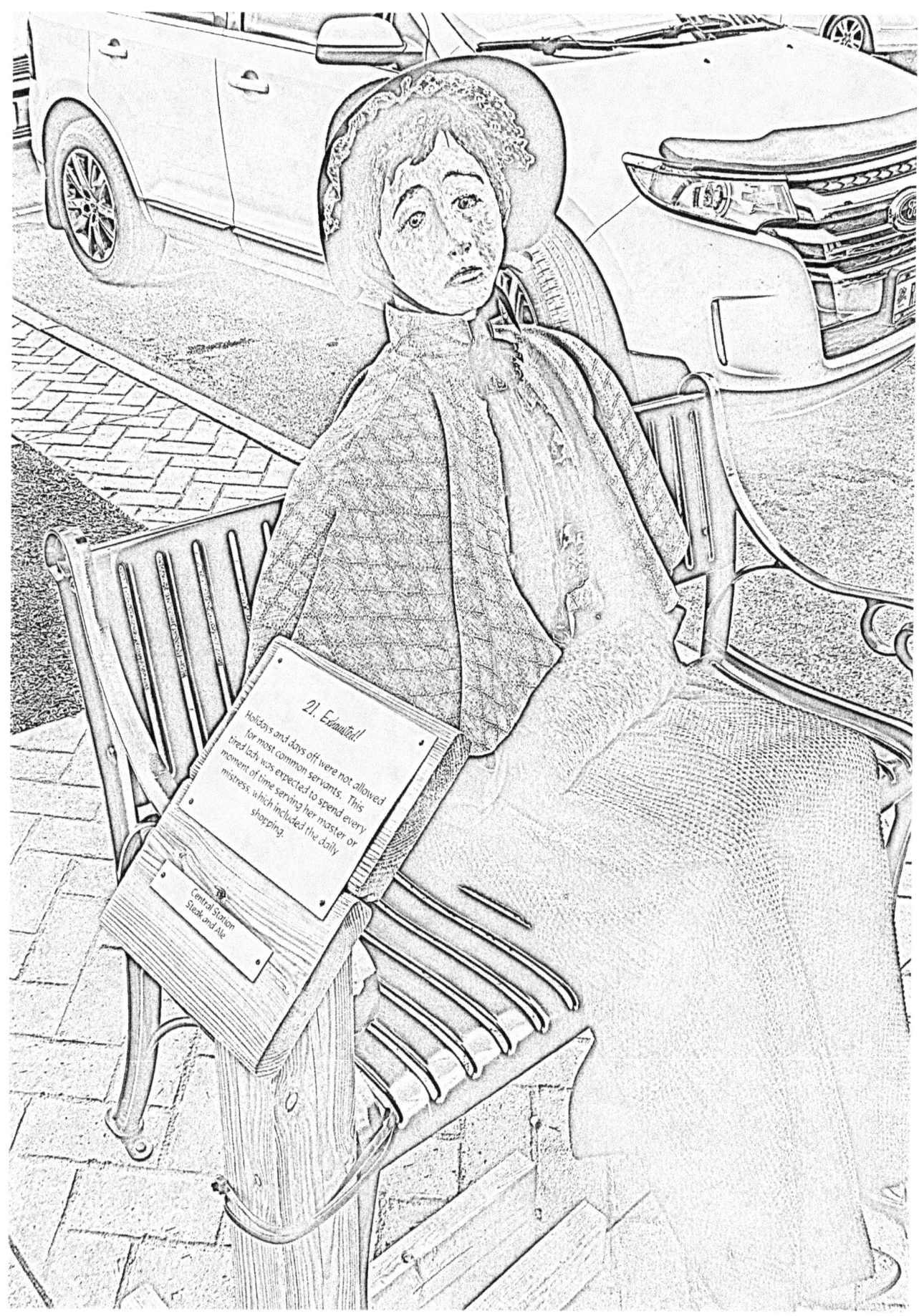

21. Exhausted!

Holidays and days off were not allowed for most common servants. This tired lady was expected to spend every moment of time serving her master or mistress, which included the daily shopping.

Central Station
Steak and Ale

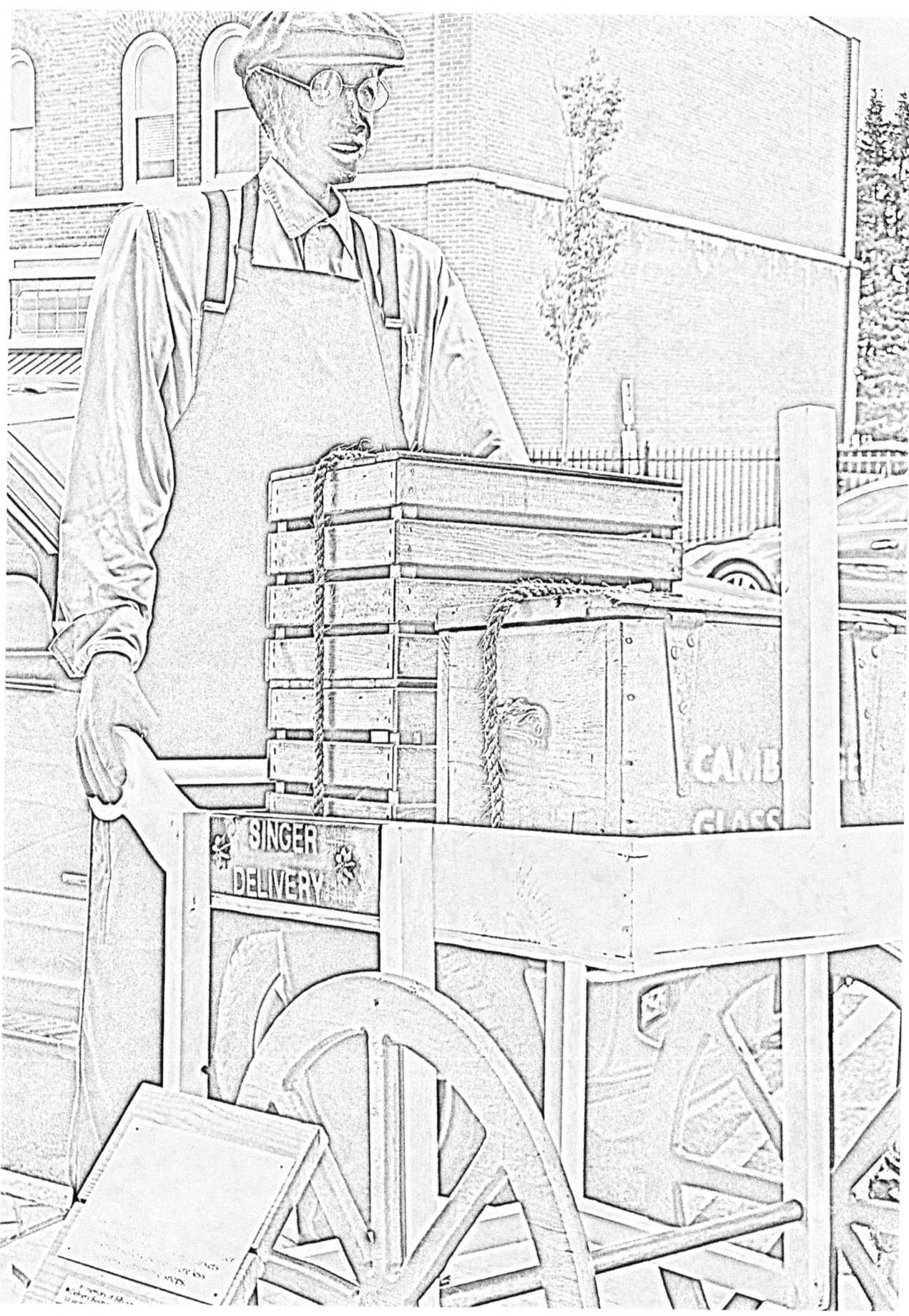

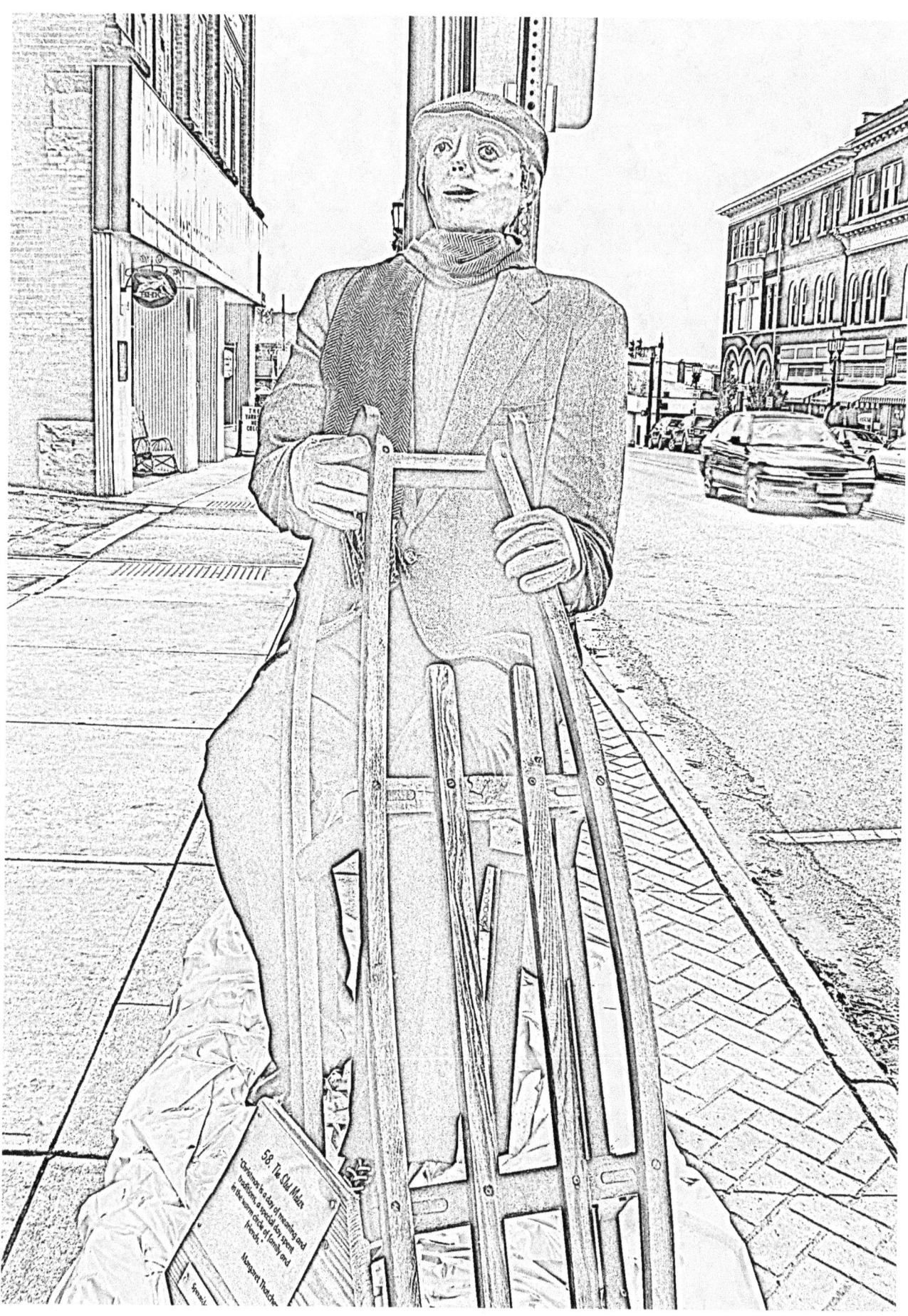

58. The Old Man

"Christmas is a day of meaning and
traditions, a special day spent
in the warm circle of family and
friends."

Margaret Thatcher

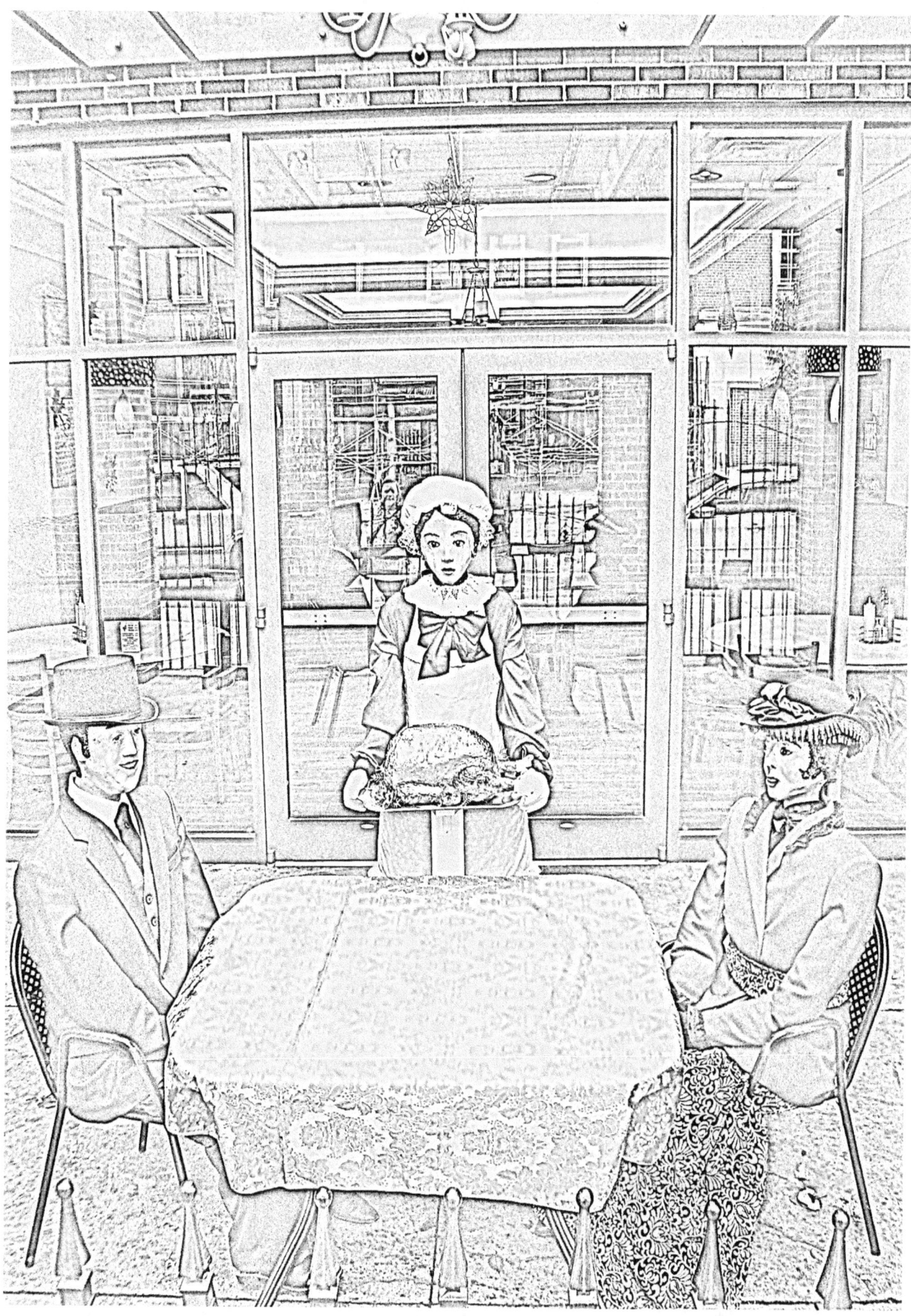

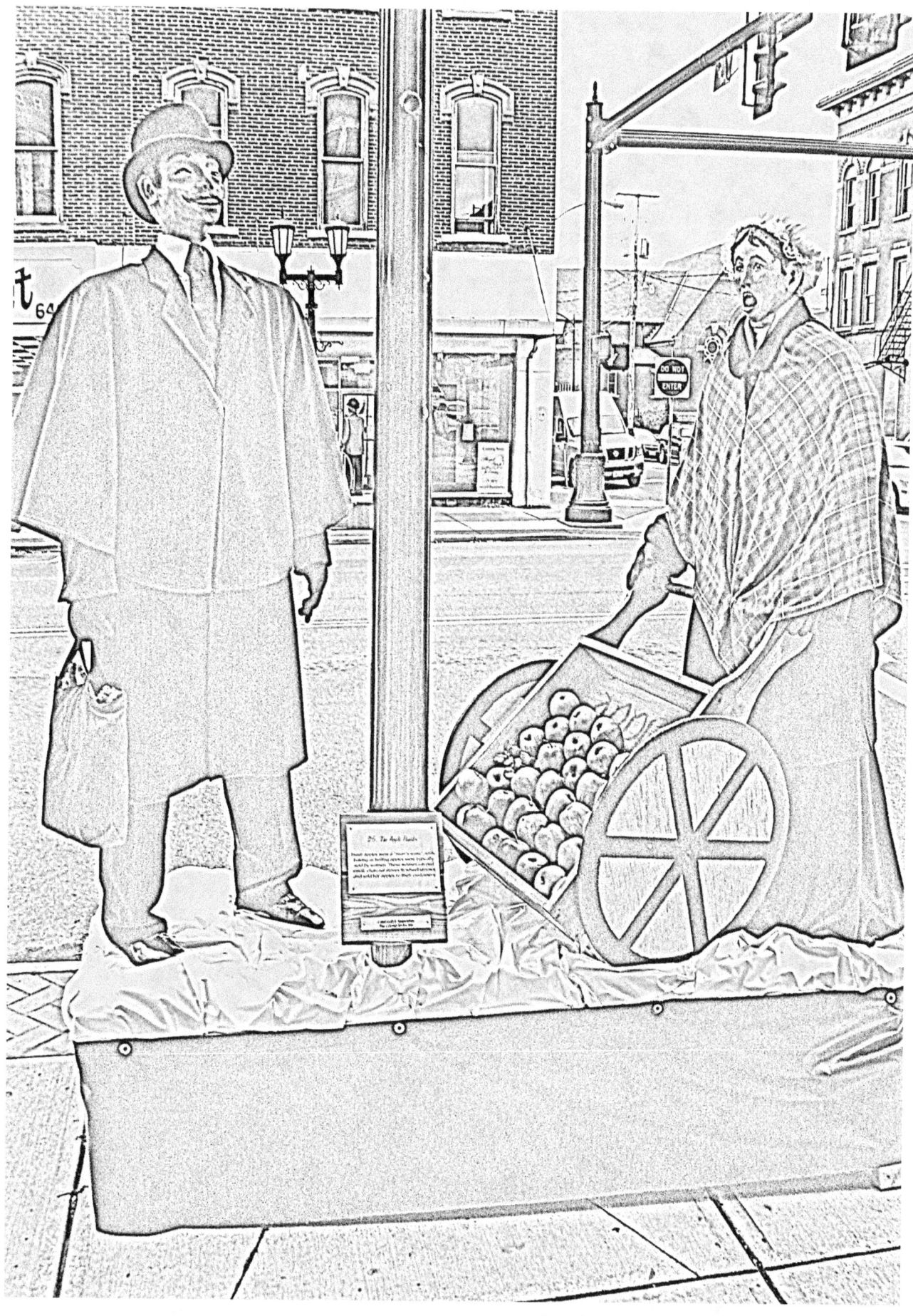

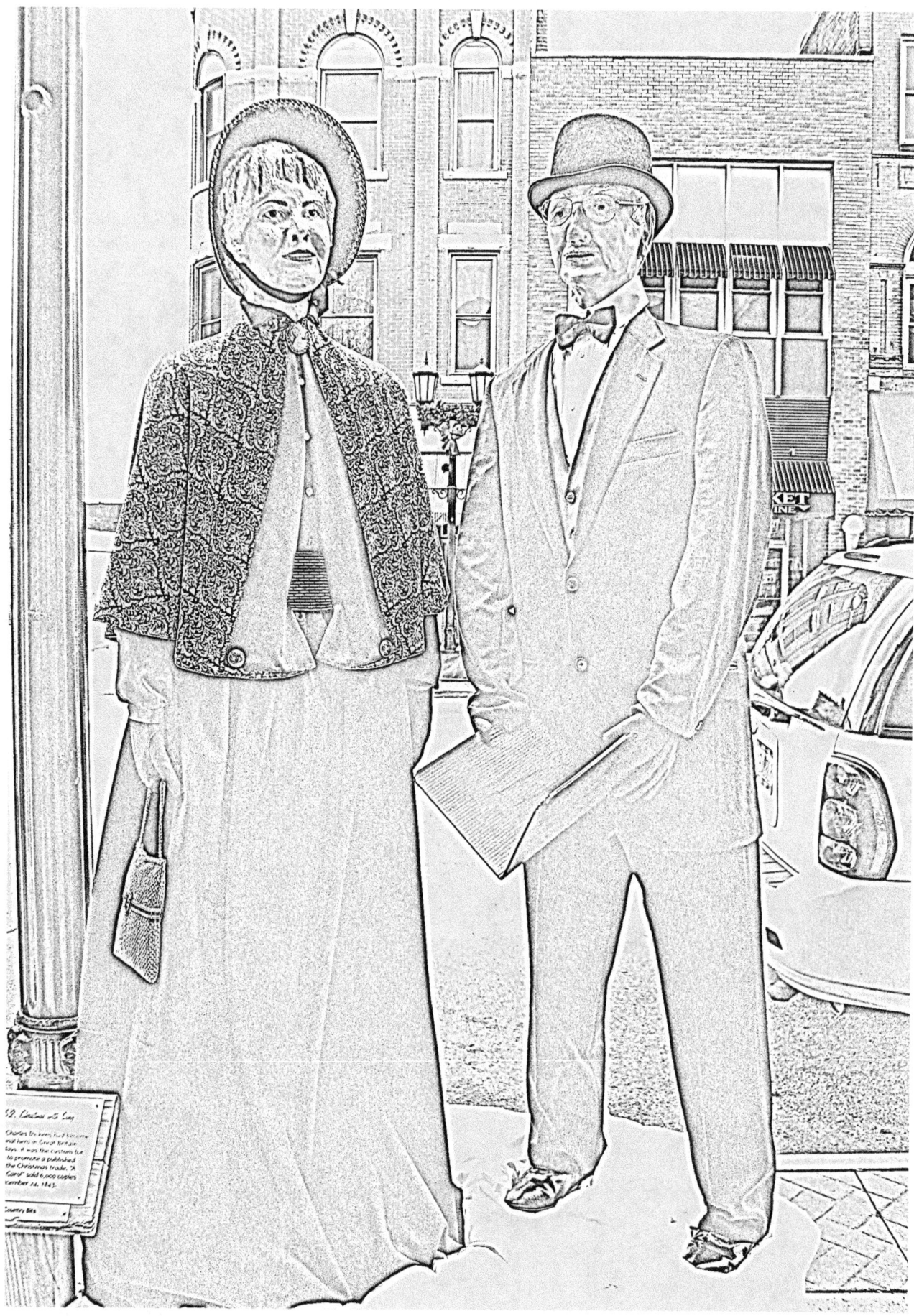

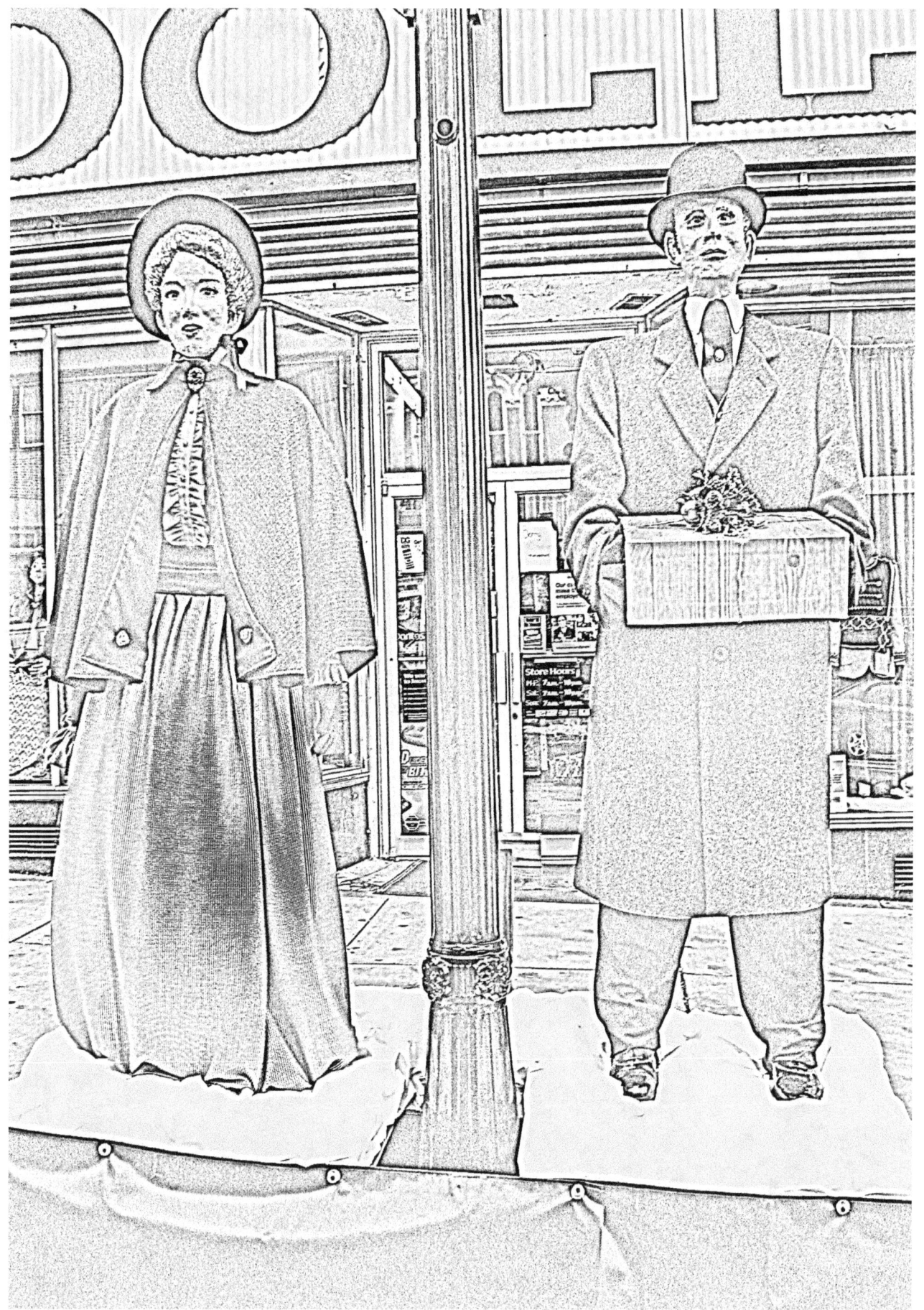

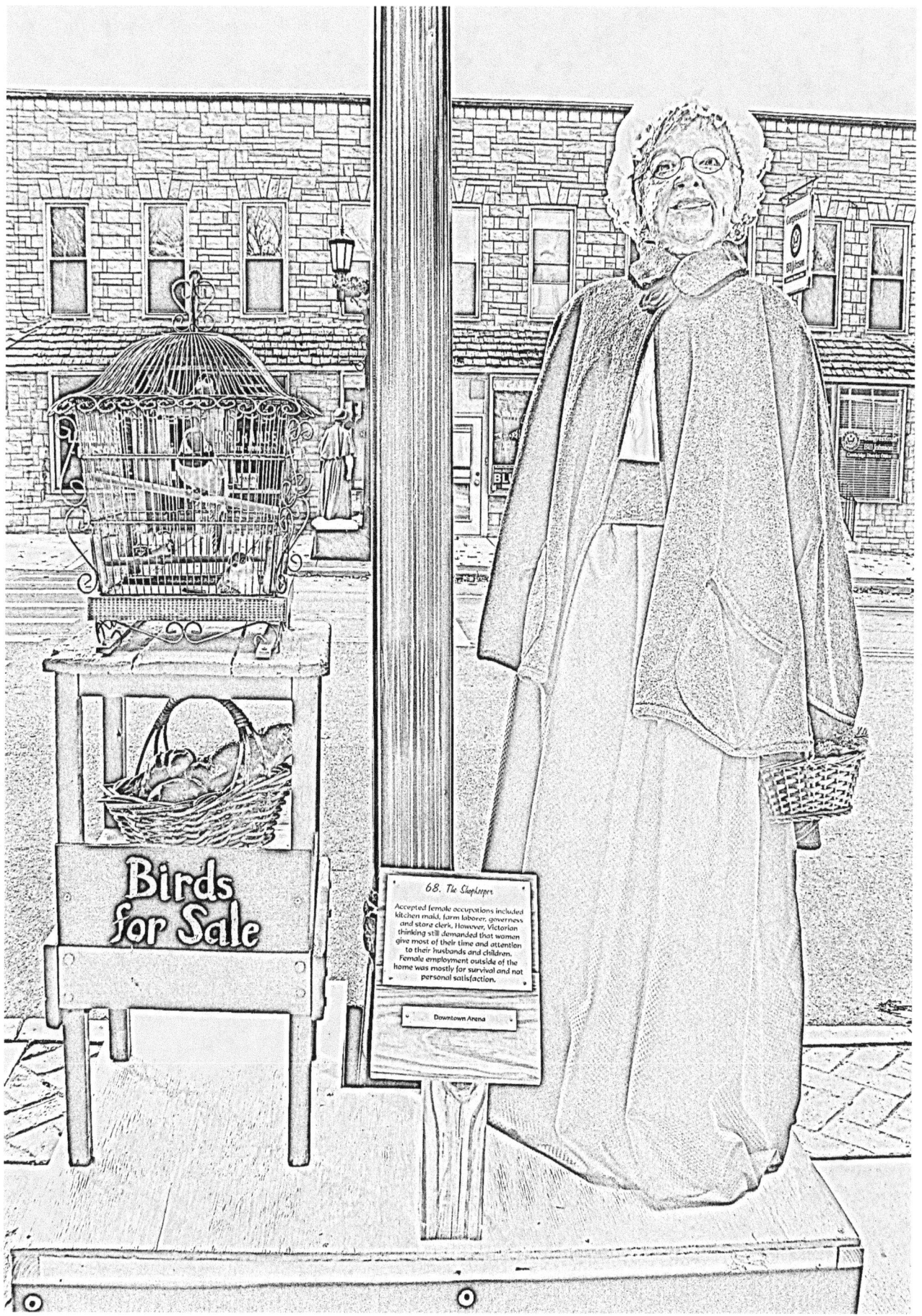

Birds
for Sale

68. The Shopkeeper

Accepted female occupations included
kitchen maid, farm laborer, governess
and store clerk. However, Victorian
thinking still demanded that women
give most of their time and attention
to their husbands and children.
Female employment outside of the
home was mostly for survival and not
personal satisfaction.

Downtown Arena

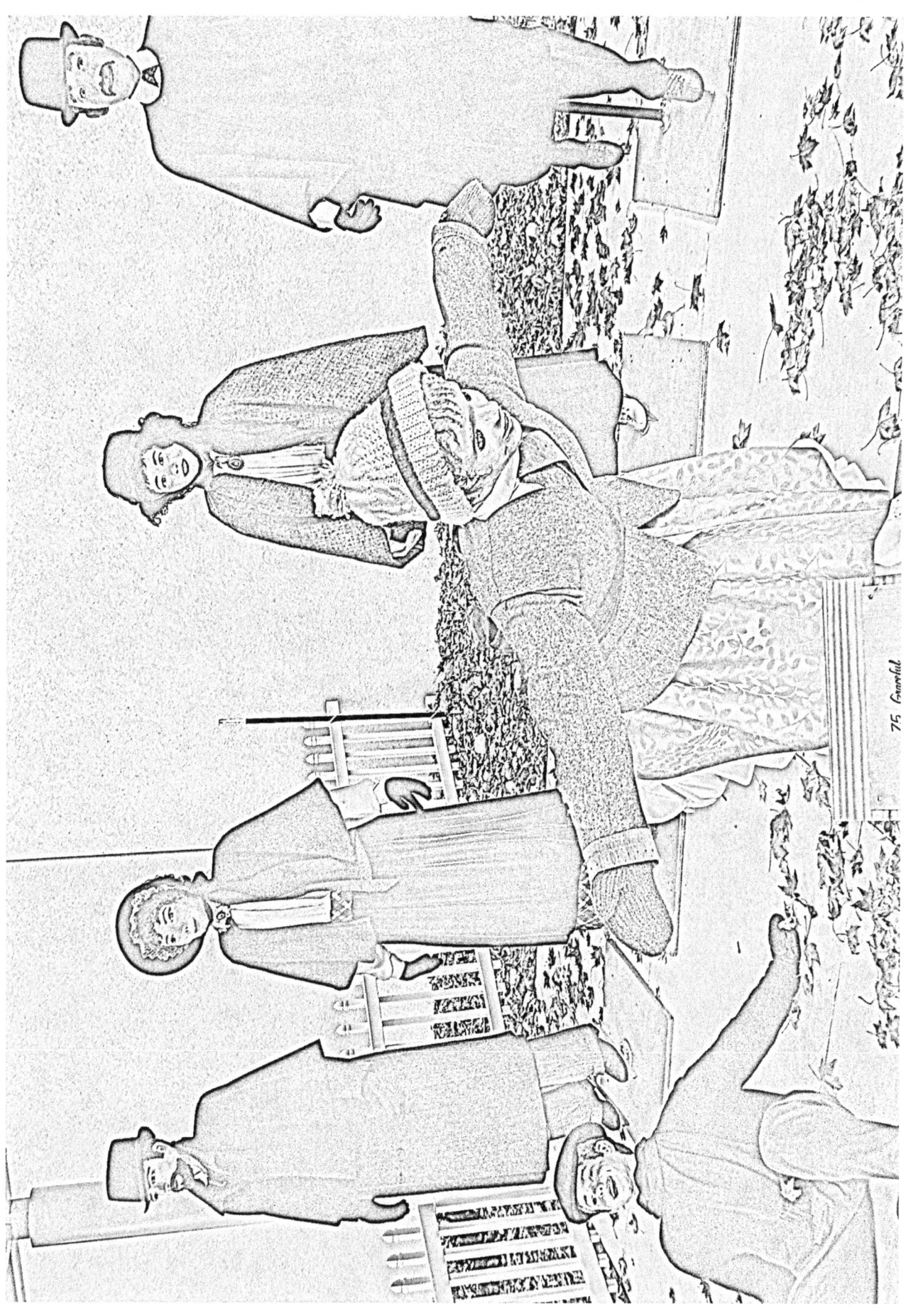

75. Grateful

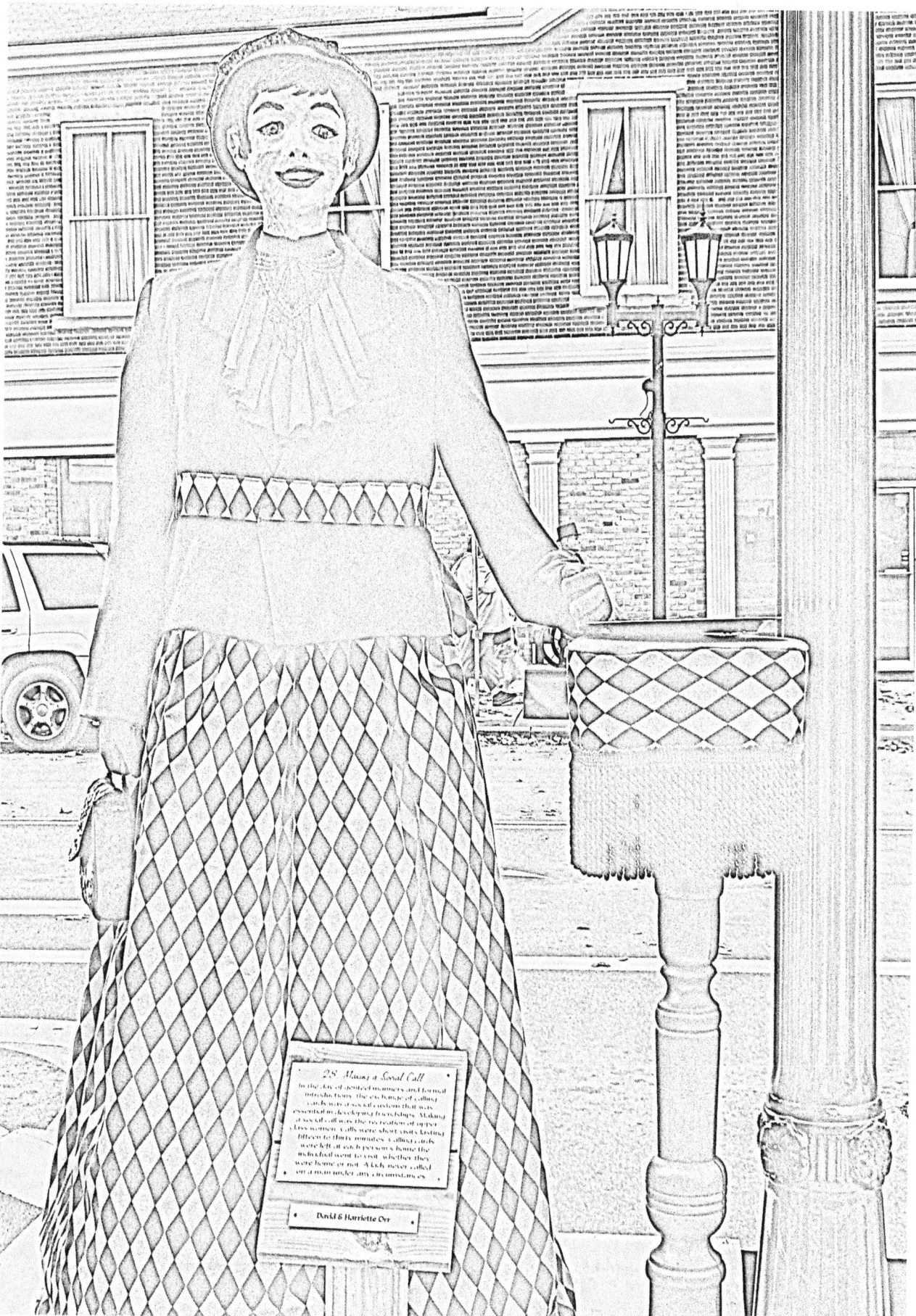

28. Making a Social Call

In the day of genteel manners and formal
introductions, the exchange of calling
cards was a social custom that was
essential in developing friendships. Making
a social call was the real vocation of upper
class women. Calls were short visits lasting
fifteen to thirty minutes. Calling cards
were left at each person's home the
individual went to visit, whether they
were home or not. A lady never called
on a man under any circumstances.

David & Harriette Orr

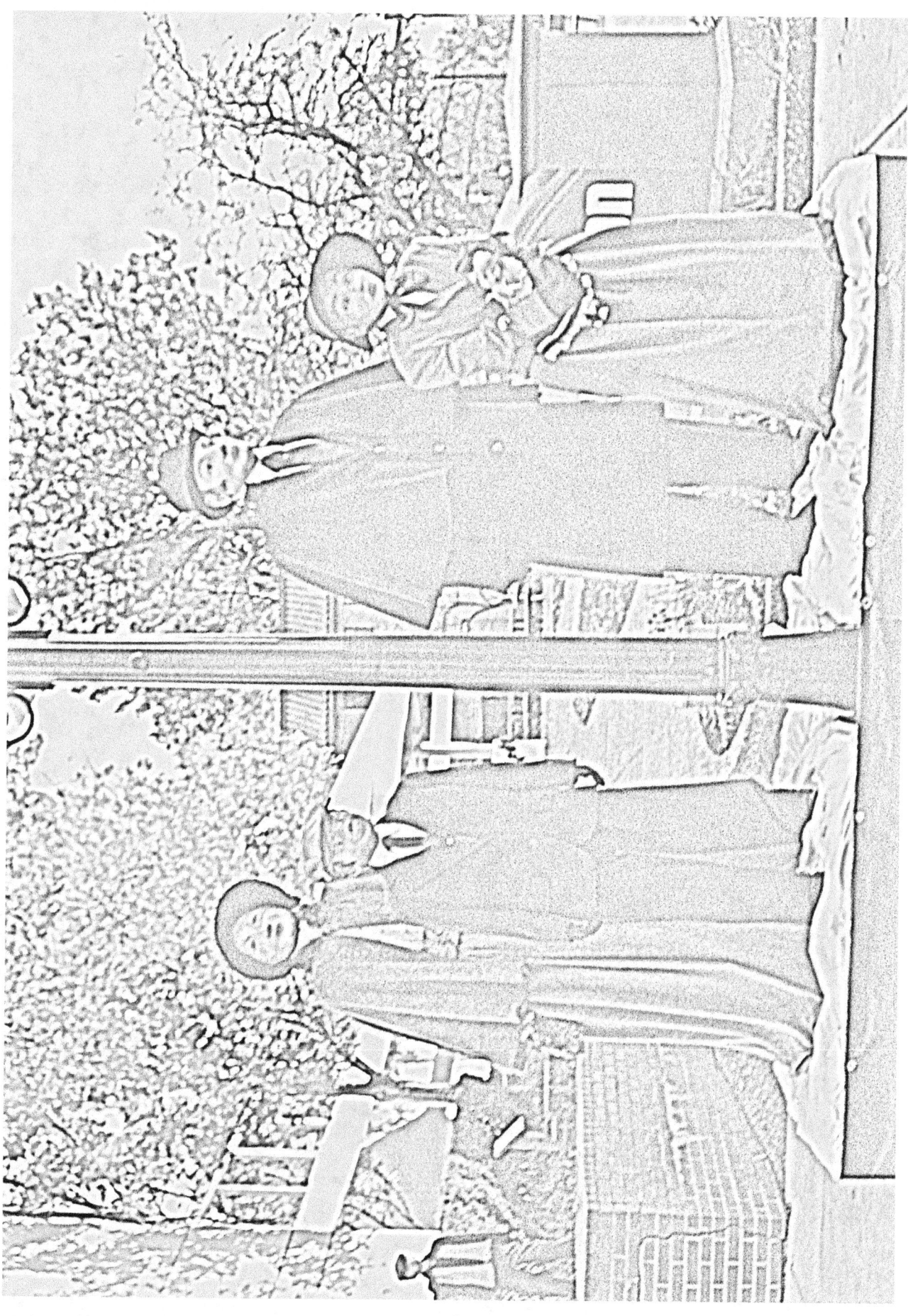

Thank You!
We hope you enjoyed our coloring book!

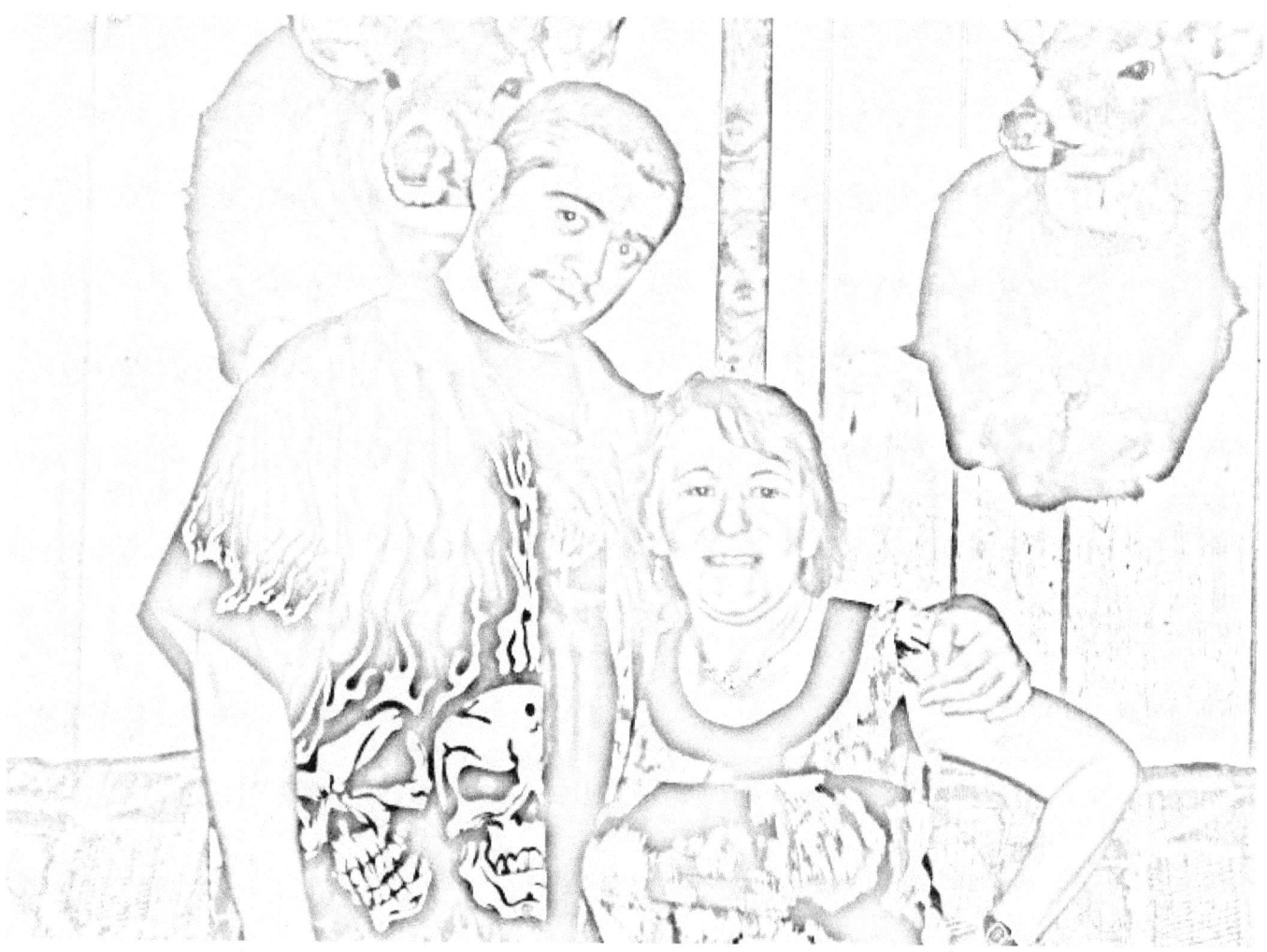

Look for more coloring books by ARN Arts LLC.
http://arnarts.wixsite.com/books